Fifty Years within
Station Limits

*My gratitude and love to my wife and daughters
for all their help and encouragement*

Fifty Years within Station Limits

THE LIFE OF A SOUTH WALES RAILWAYMAN

John M. Morgan

First impression: 2014

© Sheila Morgan & Y Lolfa Cyf., 2014

Cover design: Y Lolfa

ISBN: 978 1 84771 829 7

Published and printed in Wales
on paper from well-maintained forests by
Y Lolfa Cyf., Talybont, Ceredigion SY24 5HE
e-mail ylolfa@ylolfa.com
website www.ylolfa.com
tel 01970 832 304
fax 832 782

Contents

Foreword

CYMER AFAN, AT one time, was quite an important junction where three companies met: the Great Western Railway, the Rhondda and Swansea Bay Railway and the South Wales Mineral Railway (later to be called the Port Talbot Railway).

To gain access to the Afan Valley which is very narrow in places, the companies (or their forerunners) had to construct three long tunnels: Tonmawr (1,109 yards long), Cymer (1,591 yards long), and Rhondda (3,443 yards long). There was also a smaller one in Cymer – Gelli tunnel (169 yards long) and two substantial viaducts over the Afan river at Cymer: one of iron with dressed-stone pillars and a seven-arched one built mostly of dressed stone.

For a short period during the First World War this viaduct was guarded against saboteurs by about six soldiers of the Lancashire Fusiliers. The Rhondda and Swansea Bay Railway had stabled an old railway coach near the stop-block of the dead-end siding by the station end of the over-bridge, for the soldiers' quarters. I was told about this by my father who was living close by and I struck up a friendship with these troops.

During the 1939–45 war, the signal box windows were all covered with a gauze fabric. This had been stuck to the inside of the windows to prevent the glass from shattering into small pieces, in the event of an explosion. The Cymer Afan and General signal boxes also had a small air-raid shelter in them, for the signalmen to get into should there be an air raid. These shelters were made from steel plate, approximately half inch thick, six feet high by three feet by three feet, with cut-out slits of two inches by half an inch, for the signalman to look out of, a wooden seat inside and an escape flap on top, in case the shelter should be blown over onto its door after an explosion!

On occasions I would mention to my family about the amount and variety of work that took place at Cymer Station during my working lifetime there. Their response was always the same, "You should keep a record, and write it all down." So I have.

To have a job on the railways in those days was a job for life. It meant security for the workers and loyalty, therefore, to the employers. The free passes and privilege tickets opened up the whole of Britain to the workforce. A job worth having!

The final chapters of this book relate to this and to the warm Welsh wit and camaraderie that existed then. From my own point of view, work during those times was hard but pleasurable for all that.

I am now 78 years old and think – in fact know – that I am the last remaining person to be able to claim that I worked at most, if not at all of these different posts mentioned in the following record, at one time or another.

Finally, I would like to thank all my workmates in all departments of the railway industry who I have worked with over the years, for making it an enjoyable experience, so much so that my half-century has flown by.

John M. Morgan
(1931–2010)

Sadly, John passed away before the publication of this book.

1

Railway Stories

I<small>T WAS ON</small> 6 September 1945 that I started my railway career as a lad porter at Cymer Afan Station. I was 14 years old and had left Cymer Afan Senior School the previous July. My take-home pay at the time was £1.13.8d. (£1.68p) for a 48-hour week. Prior to me starting, I had to go to the Divisional Office in Swansea High Street for an interview and eye test. (This eye test was done by picking out and matching different coloured wools.) When I got there, the first thing I was asked by my interviewer was, "Why was I there?" I said, "To look for work, sir." He replied, "Take my tip, boy, never look for work as it will always find you!" And looking back on it – he was right! But I've got to say 99 per cent of it was enjoyable. I had to hand in two testimonials, which I had from my old headmaster, Mr Saunders, and from the vicar of my church St John's, the Rev. Tomkinson.

It had been a foregone conclusion that I would work on the railway when I left school, as my father had been working for the Great Western Railway since the 1920s and, at the time, was a signalman at Cymer Afan box. He had put my name down for a job prior to me leaving school. I had one ambition in school: that was to leave and start work on the Great Western Railwya I used to look out of the geography classroom window and watch the train movements at Cymer Station and wait for July 1945 to come and for me to start work. I already knew the time of the passenger trains, as did most of my friends. When we

My father W.J. Morgan at work

were young and out playing, these trains used to be our guide as to when to go home for dinner or tea etc., as we didn't own a watch between us! I also knew the shunting movements, as I had spent hours with my father in the signal box.

I was considered one of the lucky ones to have started on the railway – the other work available at the time was mostly in the coal mines, at Duffryn Rhondda, Westend, Glenavon, Nantewlaith, South Pit, North Rhondda and Avon; or with the Glyncorrwg Urban District Council or the C.W.S. shop; in wagon repairs, or with the South Wales Electricity Board or in forestry.

To work on the railway was a lifetime's job; there were no strikes – and you also had the benefits of privilege and free travel tickets. When I was in school, I can't remember any of my friends going away for holidays. They used to ask me what it was like to go on an express train. I used to go away every year with my parents – to Blackpool, Salisbury, London or Oxford – and stay with friends or family.

The first visit to a signal box that I can remember was to Blaengwynfi West. It was a disaster! I was about eight years of age – my father was working one Sunday and he took me to work with him. I can sense the smell of the box now, with the coal fire, polished levers and brass, and black-leaded frame and fireplace. He decided to take me across the river Afan to see the ruins of Scatton Colliery, opposite the signal box. As we got halfway over the old footbridge – only the rails were left – I fell in the river! The only bit of me that remained dry was my right arm where my father had held on to me. I spent the rest of the shift in the box, drying off by the fire, covered in the fogman's coat – complete with its red collar – which was always kept in the box ready for when the fogman reported for duty.

From Blaengwynfi West my father went to work at Glyncorrwg box in 1940. I used to go to work with him, now and again, and he would allow me to operate the small levers that used to open and close the crossing's wicket gates. So it was understandable how my ambition in life was to become a signalman, like my father – it was an interesting, responsible and secure job and most villages had two signal boxes at that time.

In September 1945, I reported for duty to the station master, Mr G.H.E. Pointer, at 09.00. He told me I was to have one week's learning duties and for the rest of that week I would be working 06.00 to 15.30 with the meal breaks between 09.00 and 09.30 and then 12.30 to 13.30, six days a week. The station master gave me a form to fill in with my measurements for my first uniform. I sent it off but had to wait six months before it arrived. So, in the meantime, to show I was a part of the team, I had to wear one of my father's Great Western Railway caps. This was much too big for a 14-year-old boy. To try to solve this, I would fold a large 'Examine Load' wagon label and place it inside the rim of the cap so that it would, more or less, fit.

I must have looked like one of the Russian officers you see on TV today! Everything would be OK for a while, but the cap would gradually loosen again and, if my hands were full, I would twitch my head to get the cap peak back to the right place again. I got so used to doing this that I would still be doing this twitching movement when I didn't have my cap on, out of work hours! It took me a long time to get out of this habit. I can remember going by bus to Porthcawl to see the firework display and, sitting behind the driver's seat, I noticed my reflection in the glass, my head twitching sporadically! So, in the end, I threw the bloody cap away!

Cymer Station at this time was a hive of activity, with all the colliers going to and from work by train, changing trains there. There was even a colliers' waiting room on the General platform, made of corrugated sheets and built around 1930 for the purpose of keeping the colliers separate from the general public as they travelled in the same dirty clothes they had been working in – no pit-head baths then. People had continually complained about the coal dust left on the seats of the public waiting room. The colliers' waiting room was pulled down about 1953 and I still haven't come across one photograph of it. I remember it because I used to clean it out at times and lit fires in there during the winter – especially 1947.

On average, 50 passengers travelled each day from Cymer to Bridgend Arsenal (Tremains) on the 06.28 and returned at 18.00. School children went to Port Talbot County, Secondary and Pitman's on the 08.10, returning 16.55; to Maesteg Secondary school on the 08.25, returning at 16.45. There were also a number of teachers travelling up on the 08.00 from Cwmafan to Cymer and Abercregan schools. Together with the above, you had packmen – men who carried their wares for sale in suitcases, and also cockle women with their wares in baskets – some of the more experienced women coping with three full baskets – one on their head and one in each hand – travelling up on the 07.05 from Swansea High Street. This train was known by railwaymen as the packman's train and arrived at Cymer Afan for Treherbert at 08.20. The last of the true packmen that I can remember was Mr Benjamin Goodman from Caerau, known as 'Benny the Jew'. Among his variety of wares, it was rumoured he also sold condoms – a very hush-hush commodity in those days! Added to all these passengers were the everyday travelling public in and out of the village.

Most of the parcels and goods' traffic for Cymer, Glyncorrwg, Blaengwynfi and Duffryn Rhondda came by rail and had to be transferred at Cymer. Milk churns and fish boxes were also carried. I have a scar on my hand from handling one of these fish boxes; it's still visible after 50-odd years. While transferring them from one train to another, the steel band around the box caught the third finger of my right hand and split it right up, with the result that I have been unable to straighten this finger ever since. I was 16 and was graded lower as a result of this injury when I went into the army. I never lost a shift, calling to the doctor's each day for a new dressing. It never occurred to me to seek compensation!

Postcard showing the hive of activity at Cymer railway station

The following commodities were also dealt with at Cymer: livestock, films for the local cinemas, flour for the C.W.S. bakery at Cymer (which was berthed at the dead-end siding at Cymer-Corrwg – to be delivered from there to the C.W.S. by the Great Western Railway lorry from Maesteg), beer for the Refreshment Rooms (the name of the station pub), all household and colliery concessional coal, coke for the schools, church and workmen's hall. This had to be weighed before delivery by the following coal merchants: the C.W.S., G. Amesbury, E.J. Miles, C. White, and D.W. Miles (Pontrhydyfen). Someone had to be by the weighbridge from 08.00 until 16.00 each day to issue the weigh tickets. All houses had coal fires in those days. All H.M. Forces personnel had warrants to travel by rail, all traffic for Nantewlaith Colliery had to go by rail, as there was no road access to the collieries and most traffic for the other collieries came by rail, too.

On Saturday afternoons and evenings the trains to Maesteg would be full, taking teenagers to Maesteg's pictures – on the 15.30, returning on the 20.50. 'Swingers' to the dance halls and pubs travelled on the 19.20 and returned on the 23.50 – known as the 'Rodney' train, the theory being that only Rodneys or ne'er-do-wells stayed out until 'all hours'! When this train arrived at Cymer the local police would be there to meet it, as there were so many passengers on the train and a lot of them had had too much to drink and were liable to start a fight over anything! That was the reason a wooden, sliding gate was put at the bottom of the steps of Cymer General platform in 1947, to control the number of passengers so that you could collect each one's ticket. But there would always be a few who would get away without paying by running across the lines by the signal boxes.

The platform staff comprised of one working foreman and

two female porters on each shift, two lad porters on day shift and a female relief porter to cover any vacancies at Cymer and Blaengwynfi. The booking offices were covered by booking clerks from 08.00 to 17.00, extended to 19.30 on Saturday evenings. When the booking clerks were not on duty, the foreman and porters would issue tickets etc., from 06.00 to 08.00 and from 17.00 (19.30 on Saturdays) until the last train – the Rodney.

The names and positions of the station staff in 1945 are as follows (most of the positions remained unchanged until 1960):

1 Station Master – G.E. Pointer
1 Chief Goods Clerk – J. Marsden
1 Goods Clerk – B. Williams
2 Booking Clerks – G. Jones, M. Jones
2 Working Foremen – J. Thomas, A.S. Walker
4 Female Porters – S. White, N. Williams, Mrs McConville, M. Pinkham
1 Relief Porter – O. Jones
2 Lad Porters – C. Rossiter and myself
6 Signalmen – (three in Afan Box and three in the General Box)
2 Relief Signalmen to relieve the above boxes, the above foreman and other boxes in the district
3 Shunters
1 Carriage and Wagon Examiner.

This made a grand total of 26 and added to this were the Afan Per Way (Permanent Way) gang of five members and the General Per Way gang of five also. Once a week the signal lampman and the linesman for the area would call.

My job as lad porter was to report for duty at six in the morning and go over to Cymer/Corrwg Station to collect the Nantewlaith tickets, check all the other tickets and close the doors of the 06.20 Cymer/Corrwg to North Rhondda workmen's train, walk back to the goods shed, light the fire and sweep out the foreman's office. I would then get water for the goods office (which was opposite the station master's house – now the site of the library), light the fire there and sweep that out. Next, I would clean the waiting room and toilet on the Rhondda and Swansea Bay Railway down-platform, brush the weighbridge and the hut out and go home for my meal break. On my return I would meet the trains and help with the parcels' traffic that would arrive on the 09.00 train from Bridgend.

After the 10.00 Neath, Treherbert and Bridgend train had departed, the platform staff would report to the goods' shed where we would work on the goods' vans that had been berthed in the goods' shed that day – normally two of them – taking the Cymer goods out and putting them into the goods' shed ready for the goods' agent, Mr G. Amesbury, to pick them up for delivery, then transferring the Glyncorrwg goods into one van and the Aber/Blaengwynfi goods into the other, ready for the vans to be picked up. This work normally took us about an hour, after which we would meet the trains and I would go home again for my dinner break. If there weren't many goods to transfer, we'd either whitewash the edges of the platforms or clean the windows on the station. Returning from my dinner break I would phone up Duffryn Rhondda checkers (later made up to working foremen, c.1955) to see if there were any parcels for delivery there or for Cynonville. If there were, I'd catch the 14.15 workmen's train to Duffryn Rhondda Halt to deliver them, returning on the 15.20 from Duffryn. If there were too many to deliver in that time, I'd have to go down again the following morning. There were times when I had to deliver a sack (112 lbs) of flour from Duffryn Rhondda Halt to Mr D.W.

Morgan, the grocer, at the Post Office, Afan Road! I would finish work at 15.30.

The other lad porter, the senior one in service was, more or less, a number-taker. He started at six and finished at 15.30 also, but with different mealtimes. Later on, around 1946, they changed the lad-porters' hours to incorporate both jobs, the hours being as above for one week and then 09.45 to 18.45 the next, with two half-hour meal breaks. The number-taker would take the numbers of all loaded wagons that arrived each day at Cymer Mileage Siding, Nantewlaith and Glenavon, together with the type of wagon and whether they had sheets or ropes, entering the details on the daily and weekly wagon returns. The results of these returns were phoned in each morning to Swansea by the chief goods clerk at 10.00. We would also take the numbers of all wagons that arrived at Cymer Mileage Sidings and would advise the consignee by sending them a postcard. The number of all loaded wagons on hand would be taken each day so that the demurrage could be worked out. At that time 9d. a day was charged if the wagon had not been unloaded after three days. A label would be removed from each wagon and would be kept on a file as proof of arrival when the consignee came to sign for them.

In the summer, we'd go up to Nantewlaith on the 06.20 workmen's train and walk back to Cymer. In the winter, we'd travel up on the 08.45 bus from Cymer and, on our return to the goods shed, enter the numbers of the wagons in the books and the types of wagons would be written on the daily wagon return forms. Then we'd help in the goods' shed, meet the trains and walk to Nantewlaith Halt in the afternoon to book and check the colliers' tickets joining the workmen's train there for Cymer/Corrwg. The lad porters had to collect and fold any wagon sheets (tarpaulins) or ropes that arrived at Nantewlaith,

Glenavon or Cymer and load them into a wagon to be sent back to the depots. The lad porters were also called upon to relight any signal lamps that had gone out. The signalman could not, very well, ask the female porter to do this job, as some of these signals were very high, especially Cymer Afan up-and-down home signals and Cymer General up-home. They were high owing to there being a bridge on the approach side of the signal, blocking its view to the driver. These home signals had been placed on top of the steep embankment leading to the river and Cymer village. Another example of gentlemen's respect for women happened one evening in 1946. A passenger train arrived at Cymer from Caerau with a carriage door open. The signalman on duty at the General box advised the foreman that the mile-long tunnel had to be examined, in case someone had fallen out of the train. I was a 15-year-old lad porter on the late shift and the only adult available to do this was a lady porter named Sybil. When asked, she said she couldn't, as she was afraid to go on her own, so I was told to accompany her. We lit the Tilley lamp and walked through. Thank goodness all was clear. I thought at the time, if there had been a body and Sybil had fainted, what the hell would I have done?

I was walking home from Cymer cinema on 21 August 1948, and as I came up Cymer hill, I heard a fall of rocks. We'd had a lot of rain over the few days previous. The rumbling came from near the cutting below Station Road. I ran down to Cymer General signal box to inform the signalman, who managed to stop the 21.00 passenger train from leaving Abergwynfi.

About a month later I received a letter to report to the superintendent, Mr J.F. Taylor at Swansea High Street, where he handed me a certificate of commendation and two guineas! The next month I had to go to Swansea again to have a medical with the railway doctor, so that they could make me a permanent

Great Western Railway
Commendation

I have pleasure in informing you that the following commendation has been entered on your record of service

When you were off duty on August 21st 1948 you heard a fall of rock at Cymmer, which blocked the running line, and, by reporting the incident to the signalman at Cymmer immediately, enabled prompt measures to be taken to ensure the safety of trains.

A gratuity of two guineas is also awarded.

To Lad Porter. J. M. Morgan.
15th September 1948.

Divisional Superintendent

Copy of commendation received and newspaper report

Prompt Action. — A Cymmer boy's prompt action in reporting a fall of rock on the railway track and thus preventing a train disaster was rewarded by the authorities on Wednesday a certificate of commendation and a monetary gift. He is Mr. J. M. Morgan, son of Mr. and Mrs. Morgan, 12 Maesteg Road and is employed as a lad porter at Cymmer Station. The commendation reads: "When you were off duty on August 21st, 1948, you heard a fall of rock at Cymmer which blocked the running line and by reporting the incident to the signalman at Cymmer immediately, enabled prompt measures to be taken to ensure the safety of trains."

employee. The result of the medical, after the doctor showed me the Ishihara Plates Test, was that I was colour-blind. This came as a great shock to me as I had always thought that I had perfect vision. A week or two after this I had to report to the chief railway doctor at Paddington and he gave me a more thorough eyesight test and told me I was partially colour-blind. I asked him if I would be able to become a signalman and he said, "We'll see." This reply was always at the back of my mind whenever I thought of applying for promotion. Had he said yes or no I would have known where I stood but, as things were, I always thought, if I apply, they will look back into my record and find I was colour-blind. A bird in the hand is worth two in the bush! I have to say though, looking back, perhaps I was being over cautious but I feel I made the right decision.

The last female porter finished at Cymer Station in 1947 – their jobs being gradually taken over by the men who had been demobbed from the Forces or ex-miners with green cards. The women porters had done a man's work throughout the war, loading and unloading fish boxes, milk churns and beer barrels, used the station hand crane, sheeted and roped wagons etc.

Hop pickers from the valley used to travel to Hereford once a year in September. The railway would put an extra coach on the 07.45 passenger train from Abergwynfi and we would load up all the hop-pickers' luggage, which included trunks, wooden tea chests, pots and pans and everything bar the kitchen sink. On another occasion, there would be a load of luggage to deal with when we had drama productions at the workmen's hall. The sets would arrive by train and had to be delivered. Bullion for the Midland Bank, Cymer also arrived on a passenger train. It was held in a strong wooden safe. It had to be signed for at each change of hands. The two lad porters would put the safe on a trolley and wheel it to the bank at Station Road. The bank manager would sign for it and hand us a half-crown tip (12p) to be shared between us! How much money was in the strong box, I have no idea! Now and again a horse-box (van), attached to the back of a passenger train, would arrive at Cymer. The van would be detached on the platform so that the owner could get the horse out. The Cymer pilot would then pick up the horse-box and shunt it into the goods' shed road for it to be cleaned and disinfected. Household removals were made by using containers. Once a year, the local farmers would bring the wool they had shorn down to the station by horse and cart to be loaded into a van and sent to the woollen mill. The hand crane was used occasionally. In 1947, when the water main was renewed between Abergwynfi and Cymer, all the pipes came by rail. They had to be loaded from the railway wagons and onto lorries by using the crane. When a plastics factory opened up at Croeserw in the same year, the output from there was brought to Cymer Station and loaded onto the van of the passenger train. Later on this traffic went to Maesteg Station to be loaded up there. Quite a lot of pigeon traffic needed to be sent off or liberated during their training season too. The station dealt with a wide variety of traffic, as the railways then were the common carriers.

Train crash

On 19 April 1946, the Treherbert to Duffryn Rhondda workmen's train, pulled by T. Vale engine No.365, an 0–6–2, became derailed 100 yards before reaching Croeserw viaduct and continued with its three coaches, three-quarters of the way across the viaduct, until eventually, the coupling on the second coach broke and the engine and first coach went through the right-hand-side wall of the viaduct and down the embankment. The engine turned over a number of times and came to rest near the old woollen factory by the river. The coaches were made of wood. All that remained of the first coach were its bogies and chassis, landing a quarter of the way down the embankment, with its sides and disintegrated roof strewn further down. The other two coaches remained upright on the viaduct, more-or-less leaning against the side wall. There were no serious injuries, apart from the driver breaking his leg! There were about ten workmen in the first coach, including Mr William Jones, the signalman at Cymer General box, who was travelling to work from Blaengwynfi for the day-shift. The cause of the derailment was, apparently, due to some fault with the cant of the track, but I can remember the railwaymen and the colliers saying the train was going too fast. I was on my way to work when I heard the crash. I ran down to the viaduct. The place was in confusion – we never thought anyone would have got out of the coach without serious injury. The driver and fireman were helped out of the engine and taken down to Cymer Afan station waiting room, together with the others lightly injured passengers to await the arrival of Dr Taylor, the resident doctor of Cymer. All the main daily newspapers reported the incident. The engine remained where it was for a month or two as they were unable to pull it up in one piece. First of all, they laid rails down the embankment and dismantled the locomotive. Then, on a number of Sundays, the rail crane would pull the pieces up by sliding them up on rails and loading them onto wagons to be sent to Swindon. The biggest piece was the firebox and boiler. Number 365 was in a very poor state when she was sent back to the Great Western Railway loco works to be put together again, but she came back into service after a few months and looked a picture! As for the coach, all the woodwork was used locally for pigeon lofts, chickens' cots and for making rafts – by the children – for use on the river beneath the viaduct.

Engine No.365, crashed over Cymer Viaduct 18 April 1946

If you were near Cymer Station in the 1940s and 1950s you had the sound of steam all around you. First of all, you could hear the empty coaching stock from Tondu to Abergwynfi going up on the western line; this train returning from Abergwynfi as the Bridgend Arsenal workmen's train. This was followed by the Llangwynwyd to Cymer General workmen's train. Over at Cymer/Corrwg the workmen's coaches would have arrived from Glyncorrwg and the engine would be in the process of running around the coaches, ready to run the workmen's train to North Rhondda. On the Rhondda and Swansea Bay Railway section, the 05.45 workmen's train from Treherbert for Duffryn Rhondda would be arriving in the down-platform and the 05.40 Aberavon to Treherbert would be approaching on the up-platform. Each one of these trains would be blowing its whistle either for the home signals or the level crossings.

Together with the sound of the railways, one would also be able to hear the sound of the collieries' hooters: Nantewlaith, Duffryn Rhondda and, sometimes, Caerau. Then there were the voices and footsteps of the colliers as they changed trains, some walking over the footbridge but most going over the level crossing or underneath the wagons that were in the sidings. I remember one station master saying he was going to stop this practice and make all colliers use the footbridge to change platforms in case anyone should get knocked down. But the colliers more or less pushed him aside when he tried to stop them.

When the colliers on day-shift would return from Duffryn Rhondda, a lot of them would call into the Refreshment Rooms for a pint. Prior to the arrival of the 15.10 workmen's train from Duffryn Rhondda, the landlady, Miss May Davies, would pull about twelve pints and have them ready on the counter as the colliers entered. On pay days and festive days the men would stay longer in the Refresh (Refreshment Rooms), catching the later passenger train to Maesteg in preference to their own. Miss Davies would fill a lot more pints in readiness on these days to save some time as she was the only one behind the bar and was getting on in years.

2
National Service in Egypt

UNTIL I WAS called up for the army under the National Service Act, Cymer Station didn't seem to change very much. It was the hive of the village. There was always some movement there, either the passenger trains or shunting movements. The lights were always on in the signal boxes – apart from 03.15 on Sunday until 03.00 Monday, when no trains ran through the village, except ballast or special trains when booked. (The Bridgend Arsenal workmen's train did run on Sundays during the war.)

I left Cymer on the 08.25 passenger train for Bridgend on 6 December 1949 to the sound of exploding railway detonators – my send off to the army from the signalmen, who would use up any old ones for any railwayman going to the Forces or on their honeymoon. I thought at the time 'I wish I was going on the latter!' My destination at the time was 9th Training Regiment of Royal Engineers, Southwood Camp, Cove, Farnborough, Hampshire. I had tried to get into the Royal Marines, to follow my father's stepfather, Mr Reuben Appleby, who had served in the Royal Marines Light Infantry, before and during the First World War. But I was told I'd have to sign on for five years with a further seven years on the reserve or vice versa. No way was I going to do that! Eighteen months were enough for me. But this was increased to two years and three years on the supplementary reserve in 1950. So, I asked to be put in the Royal Engineers as I knew they had a railway transportation unit.

I also had a form from my employer to help get me into this unit. During my basic military training at Cove we did a course on field defences, watermanship, bridge building and demolition. After the passing out parade on Tuesday, 14 March 1950, I was posted to the Royal Engineers' Railway Operating Unit at Longmoor near Petersfield (see *The Longmoor Military Railway* by D.W. Ronald and R.J. Carter), to train as a blockman – the army equivalent of a railway signalman. The cardinal rule of absolute block-working is, not more than one train may be allowed in one block section, on the same line, at one time. On single lines they use either a staff/token or One-Engine-in-Steam (O.E.S.) key. The O.E.S. key is a visible and tangible authority given to the driver to occupy a single-line section. It has the names of the signal boxes inscribed on it. If there is an intermediate ground-frame in the section, for example, Cymer Tunnel, Glenavon, Cymer-Corrwg, the O.E.S. key will release these points in the section. The signalman at either end of the section can only get one token or staff out at a time for the section (with the O.E.S. key, this was only used for dead-ends, e.g. Glyncorrwg-North Rhondda and Gelli ground-frame to Avon Colliery situated below the Graig houses and end of branch line).

I can remember my signalman father, W.J. Morgan, telling me that on many occasions when the tablet instrument would fail, the signalman would take the brass back off the clock and place it on the pouch where the tablet would normally be put, so that they could open up the pilot working on the first train. This would save the delay of a man walking from Cymer to Blaengwynfi and vice versa.

When we started the course, we were told that whoever had the best results would be staying at Longmoor, to train others coming in. Now, this suited me as my grandmother lived close by and an aunt and uncle not too far away. I had army travel warrants, plus my railway privilege and free tickets. I knew I could make good use of these on any weekends off, but I was in for a shock.

The course consisted of two weeks spent learning rules and regulations at the signalling school, then learning duties under supervision at the different blockposts: Oakhanger, Whitehill, Two Range, Woolmer, Longmoor-Downs, Weaver's Down and Liss Forest Road; then back to the signalling school for the test. I came second! We waited for our postings, during which time we were sometimes told to clean and coal the locomotives. The biggest loco at the depot was Gordon – a 2–10–0, total weight 133 tons. The Longmoor Military Railway also ran a passenger service every hour from Longmoor to Liss Station, which we called the Bullet.

My posting came through on 9 June and, guess what? It was for Egypt! The 10th Railway Squadron Royal Engineers, Adabiya Bay Camp, Middle East Land Forces 16. So the top five went to Egypt, the next few went to Germany and the one with the lowest marks stayed at Longmoor! On returning to camp after our fourteen days embarkation leave, we left Longmoor on 13 July for the transit camp at Barton Stacey and remained there until 18 July – my birthday. During the few days we were there, we noticed a few sappers who had the same arm flash [???] – a camel – as we had been issued with. They had just returned from the 10th, to be demobbed. We asked them what it was like there. Their reply was short and to the point, "F*** your luck, mates!"

We left Barton Stacey and spent the night in London,

sleeping at Goodge Street's deep air-raid shelter. Next day we went by troop train to Liverpool Docks to board the troop ship S.S. *Empire Halladale* and left there on 19 July for Egypt, calling at Tripoli and Tobruk on our way to Port Said, where we docked on 31 July. From there, we travelled by train to Ismaïlia and then by lorry to Moascar, staying there for two days before leaving for the 10th – the southern-most British Army camp in the Canal Zone – by lorry.

When we were passing Suez and approaching Adabiya Bay camp, we realised that what our informants at Barton Stacey had told us about our posting was correct! We were passing the Shell oil refinery and the smell of the fumes coming out of it was foul. On our left-hand-side was the Gulf of Suez and on the right-hand-side you could see Ali Pasha's fertilizer factory in the distance and the bare, barren mountains of Gebel-el-Ataka. In between was sand and gravel, with no vegetation apart from a few desert bushes.

We passed the Royal Army Medical Corps stores then, through the small hamlet of Ataka. Further along on the left, we passed the Adabiya and Ataka Military Railway, then Chequers Yard, the docks and another mile to our destination, the 10th Railway Squadron, by the side of the Red Sea.

We were very impressed at the smartness of the guard at the main gate, which we knew would be one of our duties in the near future. One advantage we discovered on arrival – you could no longer smell the fumes from the oil refinery – the smell of the sea overpowered it. We had to report to the commanding officer, Major G.C.L. Alexander the next day and he welcomed us to the camp and asked a few questions, the last of which was, "Have you thought about signing on to become a regular?" My reply was, "No, sir," and in my thoughts were, "What a bloody hope you've got! I'm out of this place as soon as possible!"

Our day would start with the duty bugler sounding the reveille at six in the morning; then the cookhouse call at 06.30. The next call would be a quarter of an hour to get dressed before morning parade and roll call. The duty buglers worked 24 hours on duty and 24 hours off. They were also the medical orderlies and slept in the medical inspection room which was opposite the guardroom at the main gate. Anyone who required an early call, before 06.00 – owing to early train working, cookhouse duties etc. would see the guard commander the night before and he would enter your name, time and tent number in his book. If it was you, you placed a towel on your bed as an indication to the stickman. On waking, you were required to sign his book.

Morning parade and roll call was at 07.30. Anyone who wanted to report sick would line up at the same time and be taken by army ambulance to see the medical officer in Suez. This parade was taken by the duty officer and squadron sergeant major warrant officer G.V.B. Harris, known to his men, unofficially, as 'Bomber'. He was six feet one-and-half inches in height, of military bearing, strict but fair. I can always remember him calling out on one morning parade, to all men whose khaki drill shorts were more than three finger widths above the knee, to get them lengthened, as he didn't want "any fairies in 10th Railway Squadron"!

When Bomber returned to Britain after completing his python (three-year posting abroad), Staff Sergeant Lloyd took over as acting sergeant major until warrant officer C. Woolford arrived. He had the longest waxed moustache I have ever seen! You could even see the tips of it when he was marching away from you. Apparently, when he was on the troop ship coming out, a message was put over the Tannoy advising all men who had moustaches over 14 inches long to wear navigation lights!

When morning parade was over and the men had been given their duties, a train would be waiting outside the main gate of the camp (where they also held the locomotive naming ceremonies) to take all men working on the railway to Chequers Yard and, after working there, we would return to camp by Wickham car – if one was available – or otherwise march back, for our dinner.

The Adabiya and Ataka military railway was about five miles long, from the army docks at Adabiya to our sidings at Ataka, where we would exchange our traffic with the Egyptian State Railway to and from the Canal Zone. It had two block posts – Ataka and Chequers East. (They also built one at El-Sadat Junction in 1951, but I don't think it was ever opened.) It was single-line worked, most of the time with one engine in the steam system. The junction at El-Sadat took the single line to our camp and south to Sandy Bay. The block posts had no levers inside and made use of the flag board system and line clear message, telephone and tickets and were only opened when extra traffic warranted it, i.e. when the Egyptian State Railway would run their trains down to Sandy Bay for phosphates for Ali Pasha's fertilizer factory or when extra traffic was required for the docks.

Most of my time at the 10th Railway was spent on duties other than my army trade of blockman. For three months, I was sent on detachment to the Royal Army Service Corps camp at El-Kersh, situated by the side of the Suez Canal, three miles north of Ismaïlia, where our squadron Per Way was putting in a new layout for the Royal Army Service Corps stores. When this was completed we went back to Adabiya and painted a coach in Great Western Railway colours. Our commanding officer came from south Wales – hence the choice of colours. We cleaned and painted locomotives, dealt with derailments on our railway and also at Fanara where we had a detachment, went as guards or shunters as required, together with army military duties – guards on the main gate etc.

Things changed when the Egyptians abolished the 1936 treaty and the Egyptian State Railway refused to allow our trains to run over their lines – on 9 October 1951. On Sunday, 21 October, the commanding officer, Major Alexander, called all the blockmen and two train crews into his office to tell us that we were to take over the Egyptian State Railway mainline from Ataka to Fayid the following day. The reason given was that, owing to the Egyptians refusing to move our traffic, Fayid power station was running out of oil and would be unable to produce electricity for the Canal Zone in a few days time.

The first part of the operation was to take over all the signal boxes around Suez at the same time. The line from Suez No.1 to Fayid was a double-line and a travelling blockman could be used to accompany our train from Suez No.2. Our camp could only supply transport and guards for some of the signal boxes, as our squadron was under strength. The blockmen for Suez No.1 and No.2 would have to report to the Royal Sussex Camp (which was stationed outside Suez). They would supply transport and four men as guards for these boxes. Malcolm Rhodes and I arrived at the Royal Sussex camp at 07.30 the following morning and reported to the Adjutant. We left camp by Bren Gun Carrier at 10.00 to go to our respective signal boxes. I can remember the Egyptian signalman at Suez No.1 looking out of the window as we were going over the level crossing wondering, I expect, where we were off to? I thought, you are in for a shock now, mate! Our Bren Gun Carrier slewed around the back of the box and I ran up the stairs, pointing my rifle at the signalman and motioned to him to get away from the telephones. There was also a boy of about ten years of age in the box who, I assumed, was the signalman's son. I was a bit concerned about the shock to this boy, to see his father at the wrong end of a rifle and what reaction there would be when the boy went home and told his mother. So I tried to be as friendly as I possibly could. Before the boy left I gave him some of the food I had been supplied with, so that he could take it home with him.

The signal box had a 70-lever frame: double-line block to Suez town; double-line block to Suez No.2 (to Fayid); single-line miniature staff to Fort Agrud (desert line to Cairo); single-line miniature staff to Shell (our camp at Chequers). The box also controlled the traffic for No.9 Engineers' Stores Base Depot and the Egyptian State Railway loco shed. I placed the block instruments to train-on-line and eventually had telephone communication with Suez No.2 and Shell signal boxes. The latter was quite easy because the miniature staff instrument had a box-to-box telephone incorporated within it. I was advised that our train was ready to leave, so I began setting up the road for it. I found difficulty in doing this as all the writing was in Arabic! I would look at the diagram for the numbers of the points and signals I required and, by the time I had found the numbers on the frame, I would have to go back to the diagram to recheck! Our train passed and we had to report back to the Royal Sussex camp and await orders. I returned to Suez No.1 at 17.20. At 21.00 some of our loco men from camp arrived to say they were going into the Egyptian State Railway loco shed to confiscate two of their locos which were then taken back to our loco shed at Chequers. A short while after this, an official from the American Embassy came up the box to ask if it was right that the army was taking the Egyptian State Railway locos from them, to which I replied yes and he left.

Our train arrived back from Fayid at 03.00. It was comprised of three locos and seven coaches belonging to the Egyptian State Railway which our men had picked up on the way back. These locomotives and coaches were kept at our yard at Chequers for only a few hours as, apparently, our commanding officer had been instructed to hand them back to the Egyptian State Railway.

On Monday, 5 November, I was taken to 169 (9 E.S.B.D.) at 21.00 in the commanding officer's car to pick up a train and make sure it got back to Chequers. There were not enough blockmen to man the signal boxes owing to some of them having been sent on detachment to Naffisha, and we were still waiting for replacements to arrive from the UK. We got over this as follows: I worked Suez No.1 while the commanding officer went by his Standard Vanguard staff car to Shell box. When he arrived there he gave me a release on the miniature staff instrument for that section. Our train then pulled clear of all points worked from Suez No.1 and I left the box and travelled on the train to Shell home signal. I walked from there to the box and set up the road while the commanding officer went by car to the cold storage unit to give me another release. The Egyptian State Railway had closed their box at Ataka prior to this and we had disconnected their ground frame there and clipped up the points for through working from cold storage unit to Chequers East. I arrived back at camp at 01.00.

On Tuesday, 6 November, I had to put in an early call for 03.00 so I could work as travelling blockman on a goods train leaving Chequers at four for Ismaïlia. Once past Suez No.1 we would work our trains as follows. It was a double line all the way to Ismaïlia, and I would ride with the driver of our train. If the signals were pulled off for us, we would proceed normally. If the signals were not pulled off the driver would stop the train and if the points were trailing, we would proceed cautiously.

If there were facing points I would go up to the signal box and pull off for our train. If there was a train in front of us we would continue a safe distance behind it. When we had traffic to attach or detach at Fanara, Fayid or shunt from one line to another at Ismaïlia, I would walk from the home signal to the box and work there until our train was ready to leave. On my last trip from Naffisha to Chequers, engine and van, on Saturday, 17 November, I can remember we were stopped at one station owing to the home signal being at danger. I was just about to walk up to the box, which was about 300 yards away and in the centre of the platform, when I noticed the platform was full of Egyptians who were waiting for a train. I thought, I'm not walking past that lot on my own – I'm getting a bit too near demob! I was due to leave for home in two days' time and didn't want to take any chances. I got off the footplate and pointed my rifle, No.39L8863 – this number has stuck in my mind all these years and I still have the crossed-rifles to show I achieved marksmanship at Fanara in 1950 – at the signal box and like a flash, thank goodness, the signals came off! When we passed on the platform the crowds were very hostile towards us, which was understandable, I suppose, and I wondered what the result would have been if I'd had to walk past the crowd if my bluff hadn't worked! On another occasion on the single line approaching the cold storage unit from Ataka, there was a light engine outside cold storage unit box. We could see the signals had been pulled off for the Egyptian State Railway loco to proceed to Shell signal box, but the driver made no attempt to move, with the intention of holding us up for as long as possible. So, our driver asked what he should do. I said, "Pass the home signal at danger and lift the regulator up and see what happens." It worked. The Egyptian State Railway loco made sure we did not catch up with it until we had got to Shell signal

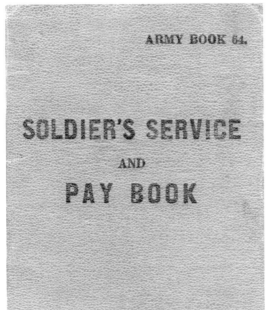

ARMY BOOK 64.

SOLDIER'S SERVICE

AND

PAY BOOK

My Soldier's Service and Pay Book from 1949 to 1951

Egyptian home for two years – the Adabiya Bay camp

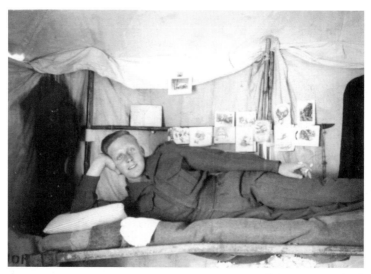

Relaxing on my bed,
Christmas Day 1950

In my uniform and
on guard

With a few of my fellow engineers

On board an Egyptian State Railways loco

Four-legged mode of transport

The Eastern
Mediterranean on fire

With Tom Rabbits
(right) in the Suez
Canal

Homeward bound with
our Discharge Books in
November 1951

box. I know these methods of working were not recommended in the military railways rule book, but I've got to say it was a very enjoyable way of working someone else's railway!

To get back to the trip – we arrived safely at Ismaïlia, then went to Naffisha and worked the engine and van back to Chequers, arriving back at camp at 17.00. Went on fire picket, got to bed at 22.00.

On Wednesday, 7 November, I got up at two in the morning and worked a goods train to Fayid, arriving back in camp at 17.30.

On Saturday, 10 November, I went to work down Chequers for 07.00. Had to go to Shell to work the signal box. Went down the Navy, Army and Air Force Institute in the evening.

The reason that we went to Shell box was because our oil (mazut) for the locos was running out and the Egyptians would not supply it to us. I crossed our train into the oil refinery. The gates leading into the refinery were padlocked across the railway. Apparently, when our train arrived at the gates, the commanding officer instructed the driver to drive the train through the gates so that our men could fill up our empty railway oil tanks with mazut.

On Sunday, 11 November, I got up at 08.00. We had a Remembrance Parade on the square at 10.45. Left Chequers at 19.30 with a double headed (2 class 8) freight train for Port Said, with instructions that I was to be the travelling blockman to Ismaïlia, where the front engine would be cut off and we were to take this to Naffisha. Another travelling blockman would meet us at Ismaïlia to work the train to Port Said. If there was no sign of the relief at Ismaïlia, we were to wait 30 minutes and if they hadn't arrived by then, we were to continue double headed to Port Said. I shall never forget this run. It was a clear, moonlit night and the sound of the steam and the movement of the footplate will stay with me for the rest of my life. I was travelling on the leading engine and the driver was doing his best to get to Ismaïlia early so that if the relief had not arrived we could complete the run to Port Said. Everything was going to plan until we got to within twelve miles of Ismaïlia. I can remember the driver asking the fireman, "How's the pot looking, mate?" "Full up!" was the reply. Port Said, here we come! About five minutes later we couldn't see each other on the footplate owing to smoke and steam coming from the firebox. Driver Pad– said, "That's f★★★★★★ it!" I said "What's up, Pad–?" and with his face down to his knees, he replied, "We've dropped a plug!" We continued on our journey to Ismaïlia where I went up to the signal box so that we could reverse the engines. In the meantime, the relief arrived so we worked the dead engine to Naffisha and had to travel back to camp by road, arriving there at 06.00.

On Wednesday, 14 November, I did some washing in the afternoon and left camp at 21.00 to work Shell signal box. No new blockmen arrived in camp yet.

On Thursday, 15 November, I went to work Suez No.1 in the afternoon and went down to the Navy, Army and Air Force Institute in the evening.

On Friday, 16 November, I left Chequers at six in the morning with a freight train drawn by a class 8 for Tel-el-Kabir. We had an armed guard of eight Mauritian soldiers on the train. On the way up, we stopped at Fanara and Fayid. We arrived at Naffisha at 13.00 where we took water and food. Before we left there, we were told we would have to leave Tel-el-Kabir before dark as nothing was allowed out of or into the garrison during the hours of darkness. We arrived there at 16.00. Tel-el-Kabir station was in the centre of the village and there were Egyptians to be seen all around the place. I walked up to the signal box which was at the end of the platform by the level crossing. To cross our train from the up to the down main and into the sidings, I had to withdraw two keys from the lever frame to operate two ground frames below the signal box. While I was doing this, the guard went up the sidings to set the hand points for the garrison. I reversed the ground frames and told the driver that when he had the sign from the guard – who was now walking back to the train – to pull the train clear of the main line so that I could put the ground frames back to normal, I would then go back to the box and replace the key for the cross-over road but retain the key for the sidings to down main, to make sure there was no delay on our return, because without this key we would have been b★★★★★d, apart from disconnecting the ground frame. The train started off and just as the van was about to clear the up main it came to a stop. I could see the driver walking back, so I went up to meet him and he told me that the engine was off the road – all wheels – with the result that our train, with 24 wagons on, was blocking the up and down main, the sidings and the level crossing! And the funny thing was – suddenly, you couldn't see an Egyptian anywhere! One of them had half-cocked the hand points. He has probably related to his children how he had one-up on the British army! He can have my best wishes now but I wished him hell at the time, owing to the trouble he caused! I had to leave the train and walk to the garrison – about a mile – and advise the R.T.O. so that he could get in touch with our operating superintendent. We couldn't get a direct connection on the phone – we had to relay our messages through the telephone exchange at Ismailia. I can remember asking the telephonist, "What was his reply?" and he said, "Tell Morgan that if anything is missing from that train, he'll never see demob!" Just because I was the only non-commissioned officer and a lowly lance corporal at that, on the train. A proper gentleman was Q.M.S.M. Eddings! I remember that he had malaria once and I was sent up to his tent to pack his kit ready for him to go to hospital. When I got back to my tent, I told the boys, "Q is looking very ill!" Their response was, "We hope the b★★★★★d dies!"

To get back to Tel-el-Kabir. I had to leave the garrison by armoured car to return to the derailment. One of our trains arrived with men to rerail the loco but when I left for Naffisha at five in the morning it had not been rerailed.

We had to work engine and van from Naffisha to Chequers. The driver and fireman had only just come out from Longmoor and did not know the road so I had to advise them of the position of level crossings etc. (I would still like to meet the Royal Army Service Corps's motorcyclist that we all-but knocked down at one level crossing – as I wasn't too sure of their positions either!) The driver refused at first to take the engine out, owing to bad brakes. These were readjusted but apparently, too finely, so if we were stopped at a home signal, the driver was unable to release the steam brake. He had to use the adjustable spanner to disconnect the brake in the cab. After that was done I would blow the whistle, the fireman would apply the hand brake and the driver would have to use the spanner to get the steam brake working again. In fact, it was quite an enjoyable run! When we arrived back at Suez No.1, I went up to the box and discovered that some new blockmen had arrived from Longmoor. We got back to Chequers at five in the afternoon.

On Sunday, 18 November, I packed my kitbag and went for a good wash in the sea. I then went down the Navy, Army and Air Force Institute in the evening to get tight and say farewell to some of the finest mates I have known in my life. I was looking forward to leaving for home but, by damn, I was enjoying my last night at 10th Railway Squadron! I was doing the work I enjoyed doing. I was given orders to follow when I left camp but, after that, it was up to me until I reported to my destination. You made your own rules but you made sure you still had a safety margin and there was no bullshit.

I left 10th Railway Squadron for the U.K. on Monday, 19 November 1951. I was demobbed on 6 December but went to Longmoor for a fortnight each year for the next three years. (For further reading, see *Middle East Movers* by Col. Hugh Mackintosh.) I had my army leave due to me, then I reported back to British Rail to resume my civilian job on 28 December.

3
Civilian Life again

I REPORTED TO the station master, Mr F. Morgan, at Cymer and was told to report to Swansea High Street office for an interview on 28 December where I was told there was a signalman's post at Waterhall Junction, Pyle. I didn't have transport to get there. I was also offered a shunting post at Duffryn Yard or a leading porter's post at Cymer. I decided to take the latter in preference to the other two posts as it enabled me to see more of my girlfriend, Sheila, who lived locally and with whom I had been corresponding during my army days. I started back on 31 December 1951 having been away for two years.

When on an afternoon shift, I made arrangements to swap a few hours with my fellow porter, George, for the weekly youth club nights, so that I could spend a few hours more with Sheila and walk her home afterwards. When I had been back for a few weeks, I could see that Cymer Station was not as busy as when I had left. There were not so many colliers using the trains to go back and forth to work. More use was being made of the service and contract colliery bus; a lot of school children going to Port Talbot were now using the service bus, also the ones living in Croeserw and travelling to Maesteg School. The buses were more frequent, beside which you couldn't expect anyone to walk all the way from Croeserw to the railway station when there was a bus passing their house every half hour, to and from Maesteg – and the council estate was getting bigger all the time. Nantewlaith and Glenavon Collieries had closed a few years earlier and the parcels' traffic was now being dealt with at Port Talbot Goods and delivered from there to the villages by lorry. The beer for the Refreshment Rooms now came from Swansea by lorry. Instead of the Post Office using the trains for their mailbags, they now had their own vans. Less milk and fish came by rail, the collieries now closed on Saturdays and the railways started to cut some of the Saturday trains. The first ones to go were the ones best patronised by the teenagers going to Maesteg or Port Talbot for the pictures: the 15.25 from Abergwynfi, and the 17.10 from Blaengwynfi.

I remained at Cymer as a porter until 7 July 1952. From there I went to Lower Cynon box as a signalman, class 4, and took on duty there after passing the rules and regulations with the district inspector, Mr Albert Davies; the chief inspector, Mr P. Bowen and the superintendent, Mr J.F.M. Taylor.

There were three shifts – days, nights and afternoons – no weekend working, only when required. It was a very quiet box, seeing very few people. To make my time more interesting I

Lower Cynon
signal box

did a Signalman's Correspondence Course and made myself a crystal set as, at that time portable wirelesses were quite big and the batteries didn't last long. The signal box was lit by a Tilley lamp, there was no running water – that had to be fetched from a nearby *pistyll* (spring) situated at the left-hand-side of the road, about 300 yards from the box. It was also shown on the Ordnance Survey maps. The water was always cold and a pleasure to drink. People would have great difficulty finding it now. There was no toilet, only the bushes of the great outdoors – which could be a cold experience during the wintertime – but an ideal spot and opportunity for studying birds of the feathered variety!

The layout consisted of a single-line section leading onto a double line. The box was positioned in the cutting below the steps and retaining wall that you can still see by the main road, where at one time stood an isolated house known as Beaman's, built about 1906 but derelict by 1954. The last occupant was Charlie, who was quite intelligent and had seen better times. There was also a lodger called Ezra. They would call to the box now and again for some oil for their lamp or some coal for their fire and cadge a cigarette. When they left (I assumed to be taken into care, as they both must have been old age pensioners) we missed their occasional visits. Now the only people we saw were the ganger, who was walking his length on a daily basis, and the station master, or district signalling inspector, about once a fortnight.

In the summer of 1953 and newly married, I suddenly found great difficulty in getting to the box on time when on day shift. Why this should be I do not know! My wife and I kept sleeping through the alarm and something serious had to be done about it. I decided to invent my own alarm clock which turned out to be a work of art – even if I say so myself. It never let me down, and had I been more forward thinking, I could have patented it and beaten the Japanese to the market!

Basically, it consisted of a small, wooden arm, the end of which was weighted with lead. This was put to rest on the alarm key and would drop as the alarm went off, making a connection with a car horn. It would wake the dead!

I left Lower Cynon in 1953 to go as a Swansea district relief signalman, class 2, at Cymer. This job mainly entailed relieving the signal boxes at Cymer Afan, Cymer General, Blaengwynfi, Glyncorrwg and Duffryn Rhondda, for rest days, sickness and holidays. I also relieved the porters and working foremen.

Like father like son

The job of relief signalman was very interesting, as you had such a variety of work and the time would pass very quickly. Cymer being my home station, wherever I was sent entitled me to 20p to a mile allowance or lodging allowance, depending on the distance. You would be at different places for a few

The second generation at work

days or weeks at a time. Other work I did on the relief was, pilot man for single line working from Bridgend to Stormy or Stormy to Margam Water Street or Margam Moors; hand signalman at locations between Tremains, Bridgend to Neath and the branch lines; electronic speed testing of trains at Pyle East and Pyle West (owing to a lot of derailments throughout British Railways due to short wheel base wagons, c.1963); in charge of movement and protection of the rail crane during the change of layout at Cymer and other places; taking census at level crossings; train recording at Margam East and Port Talbot Panel for three months when it opened.

During my time as a relief signalman we would, now and again, get 'spare' days when decisions as to where I'd be sent were made on the spur of the moment by my boss, the district inspector. On one of these days I was told to report to Cymer where, by chance, I had the pleasure of meeting the railway historian and photographer, Michael Hale. What he didn't know about local railways wasn't worth knowing! We became good

Cymer Afan Station, September 1957
© Michael Hale

friends over the years and it is thanks to him and the books he wrote that there are so many photographs of the whole area.

One of the stories I learnt from him added to what I had once been told by 90-year-old Mr Jones, the owner of a mine in Abercregan, about a head-on collision in Gyfylchi tunnel which occurred on Saturday, 16 August 1902. At first I hadn't believed it as no-one else seemed to know anything about it, but Michael Hale had all the details except for the numbers of the locomotives involved, though he suspected that one of them was No.4, as that loco was photographed with an industrial type of bunker. He said what happened was this:

Trains usually crossed at Cymer although it was possible to cross at Tonmawr but this had to be by special arrangement. On a Saturday, the last down-train at 16.30 from Glyncorrwg crossed the last up-train, the 16.00 from Incline Top at Cymer. On this particular day Mr Perrott, a cashier, asked for the down-train to run through to Tonmawr and cross the up-train there, instead of waiting at Cymer, so that he could get to Briton Ferry as soon as possible. The traffic manager at Glyncorrwg agreed but told the cashier to make these arrangements himself at Cymer for crossing at Tonmawr. The cashier later said that he had understood that the traffic manager was going to make the arrangements. The result was that nobody had done so.

When the driver of the down-train was halfway through the tunnel, he saw the up-train enter at the opposite end and managed to stop his train. But the up-train came on without slowing. The driver and firemen of both locos, the cashier and seven passengers were injured, two of the latter dying as a result of their injuries. Each train consisted of an empty coal truck and break van.

Regarding the problems of the single line from Tonmawr to Glyncorrwg, the electric staff system was introduced in March

1918 for the public passenger service. Previously, the line had been worked one-engine-in-steam, according to the inspecting officer. Presumably, one-engine-in-steam from Cymer.

I was working Blaengwynfi box on 7 July 1955 when Mr J. Davies, aged 78, who was a little infirm and with failing eyesight, walked in front of the midday passenger train to Treherbert. I ran to pull him off the line and the engine knocked him out of my arms, onto the up-platform. He suffered several fractured ribs and died in hospital a few days later. About a week after the inquest, I had to go to the superintendent's office in Swansea

RAIL DEATH DESPITE "BRAVE BID"

An inquest jury at Neath yesterday complimented a young relief railway signalman. John Malcolm Morgan, of Maesteg-road, Cymmer, on his "prompt and courageous action" in attempting to save the life of a 78-year-old man knocked down by a train at Abergwynfi railway station.

Recording a verdict of accidental death on Jeremiah Davies, of Jersey-road, Blaengwynfi, the deputy West Glamorgan coroner, Mr. I. E. Cameron, also added his compliments to the signalman and said that the only cause for regret was that his brave bid failed to save the old man's life.

AS TRAIN APPROACHED

William George Grist, of Gelli-terrace, Abergwynfi, railway porter, said that on July 7 Davies purchased a ticket for Treherbert and made to cross the railway track to wait on the opposite platform.

Grist said he suddenly noticed a train was approaching from Cymmer and he heard the signalman, Morgan, shout to Davies: "Stop!"

The old man did not seem to hear, but after a second shout he hesitated before again walking on into the path of the oncoming train.

"PULLED HIM BACK"

Grist said he then saw Morgan run to the old man and pull him back from the train, but as he did so Davies was struck a blow by the engine which rendered him unconscious.

Other witnesses spoke of Davies as being a little infirm. It was stated that his eyesight was failing.

Davies suffered several fractured ribs and died of pneumonia a few days after the accident at Neath General Hospital.

GLAMORGAN ADVERTISER
FRI JULY 22 1955

Signalman's courage commended by Coroner

A RELIEF railway signalman, John Malcolm Morgan, of Maesteg Road, Cymmer, was complimented by the deputy West Glamorgan Coroner, Mr. Ian Cameron, at an inquest at Neath, on Tuesday, on his "prompt and courageous action" in trying to save the life of an old man who was knocked down by a train at the Abergwynfi railway station.

The jury retured a verdict of "Accidental death" on Jeremiah Davies aged 78, of Jersey Road, Blaengwynfi. The coroner added that it was to be regretted that the bravery of this young man failed to save Mr. Davies' life.

William George Grist, a railway porter, of Gelli Terrace, Abergwynfi, said that Davies bought a ticket to travel to Treherbert and went to cross the railway track to the other platform where his train was due.

"STOP"

Grist then said that he noticed a train was approaching from the direction of Cymmer and he heard Morgan shout to the old man, "Stop!"

Davies apparently did not hear but after Morgan had shouted a second time he hesitated and then walked into the path of the train.

Morgan then ran to the old man and pulled him back from the train, continued Grist. As he did so Davies was struck by the engine and knocked unconscious.

Davies was taken to Neath General Hospital where he died of pneumonia a few days after he was admitted on July 7. He also suffered several fractured ribs.

Newspaper reports about incident

51

to be presented with a letter of commendation and two guineas gratuity.

When they put the new box at Cymer, with a new layout and a 50-lever frame, the signal box was put up to class 3 and the relief signalmen to class 1 relief. Most of the time I was able to get to the various signal boxes in my district by public transport – bus or train – apart from opening the boxes for the first train on a Monday or closing them after the last train on a Saturday when no public transport was available and I had to resort to walking or using my bicycle. One of the most difficult to get to was Glyncorrwg for the morning shift – 03.55 to 11.55, Monday to Saturday. It was only about three miles from my home – not far, but uphill all the way. Perhaps I would not have been called upon to relieve there for a month or two with the result that my first few mornings would always follow the same pattern – I would be cycling past Ynys Corrwg Farm close by the side of the road at about 03.40. Two alert, conscientious sheep dogs, wondering who the hell was about that early in the morning, would race out to investigate then chase me, barking, for about a hundred yards. I couldn't do anything to get away from them as I was peddling like mad up the hill. After a morning or two of this I would phone Mr Jenkins, the farmer, and ask him to keep the dogs in. His reply was always the same. "Don't worry, boy, they're only playful!" and I would reply "But I'm not feeling very playful at that time in the morning!" Despite this harassment from the damned sheepdogs, once I arrived at the signal box, switched in and had the fire lit, it was a nice place to work as it was in the centre of the village and people would be passing the box all day long. Having a chat now and again with some that I knew helped the time pass very quickly.

Glyncorrwg Railway Station

The staff working at Glyncorrwg
Station Master
2 Porters (06.00 to 15.00 or 09.00 to 18.00 with one-hour meal break)
2 Signalmen, class 3 (03.55 to 11.55 or 11.55 to finish)
1 Carriage and Wagon Examiner
2 Head Shunters (05.00 to 13.00 or 13.00 to finish)
1 Goods Guard (08.00 to 16.00)
1 Driver (08.00 to 16.00)
1 Fireman (08.00 to 16.00)
5 in Per Way gang
(Non-railway staff: 2 Wagon Repairers)

The station composed of a signal box, waiting room and booking office on the platform – and an air-raid shelter that was made into a Per Way cabin after the war – station master's office, goods' office, goods' shed, weighbridge and carriage examiner's cabin and also a wagon repairs' cabin. The station was gas-lit and the yard lit by means of Tilley lamps. It had a water column and, at one time, a small loco shed. The Western Welsh bus was kept in the yard overnight. Previously, the bus was kept in the garage but later this became impossible owing to bigger buses.

Parcel traffic would arrive from Cymer on the 11.00 Western Welsh bus, to be delivered by the porters. Any parcels and perishables arriving at Cymer by passenger train for Glyncorrwg had to be transferred to the 10.45 bus by Cymer porters. Apart from this, each afternoon, the porters would take out the front seat behind the driver of the 15.45 bus to put milk churns in its place for Mr Bert Gilbert, the Glyncorrwg milkman. This practice stopped about 1954 when he had to come to Cymer Station with his horse and cart to pick them up each afternoon. Any fish boxes would arrive on the Cymer pilot or the empty coaching stock from Cymer/Corrwg in the afternoon.

The signal box was opened at 03.55 until finish, approximately 20.00. (At one time it was opened for the full 24 hours, with three shifts in the box. The night shift no longer happened after 1944.) The 03.10 goods train from Duffryn Yard would be banked up and arrive at Glyncorrwg about 04.50 and pull up on the single line, clear of the points above the level crossing. After sufficient brakes had been put down on the wagons, the banker was cut off and crossed into the shed road for water, then to return the light-engine to Duffryn Yard. The brake van would be cut off and gravitated into the mileage siding. When it was clear of the points, the train engine would propel the empties into the siding, cut off and go for water. After filling up, it would then pick up the coaches from the carriage sidings, having first received the Annett's key from the signalman, to operate the ground frame before propelling the coaches into the platform, handing the Annett's key back to the signalman who would then ask line clearance to Tonmawr (later, Cymer General). The signalman handed the train staff to the driver for the train to run to Cymer/Corrwg, arriving there at 06.00. The engine would run around the coaches and leave there at 06.20, having waited for connections from the workmen's trains from Treherbert, Tondu and Aberavon. When the colliers' train had arrived back at Glyncorrwg at approximately 06.30, the engine would run around the coaches to propel them to South Pit and North Rhondda. The Glyncorrwg porter would issue tickets at the booking office. These were collected by the head shunter and handed to the signalman to be cancelled.

The third leading brake had a horn worked by a foot bellows (later, a bell) which the guard would use as a warning when approaching the level crossings above Glyncorrwg and to warn any colliers walking the line. The train was also accompanied by the head shunter, who would operate the outlet and trap-slotted spring runaway catch points by means of the One-Engine-in-Steam (O.E.S.) key, on the way back from North Rhondda and South Pit. The porter would issue the tickets and the shunter would collect them. The train would return from North Rhondda at about 07.00, arrive at Glyncorrwg 07.15 (at one time, two trips were made), then put the coaches back in the sidings, where they would be cleaned out by the porter and recharged with gas – for lighting the compartments – by the carriage and wagon examiner, from a gas tank wagon, when necessary. Up until about 1956, the coaches had wooden seats.

The engine would cross for water then cross onto the empties and the train crew would be relieved by the Glyncorrwg crew at 08.00. The Duffryn Yard crew would then catch the bus to Cymer, having first received a warrant – a piece of paper stamped with a rubber stamp made out by the porter. They would catch the 08.10 train from Cymer to Aberavon Town. The rest of the morning, empties etc. would be worked to North Rhondda and South Pit and loaded back to Glyncorrwg Yard, the train being stopped above the level crossing, the engine being cut off and standing in the platform (mainline), the loaded wagons being gravitated into the yard.

The 06.10 Duffryn Yard would arrive (a banker load, more often than not) at about 09.15, after shunting West End, putting off the loaded from there into Cymer/Corrwg sidings and putting off at Nantewlaeth, if required. The banker would return the light engine to Duffryn Yard, after taking water. The 06.10 would put off the empties into the siding, go for water, then pick up the down-line traffic for Duffryn Yard, leaving Glyncorrwg around 10.45. The Cymer pilot would arrive at 12.15 with the goods' van from Cymer goods' shed and any other traffic that had been put off at Cymer for Glyncorrwg. It would also put off traffic at Nantewlaith on the way up. The Cymer pilot would leave Glyncorrwg about 12.45 after taking water and picking up any up-line traffic. These would be put off at Cymer/Corrwg ready for the Tondu trains to pick them up. Traffic from South Pit to Nantewlaith (North End) would be worked down with the 06.10 from Duffryn Yard light engine banking the Glyncorrwg pilot, both engines returning to Glyncorrwg afterwards. At 14.00, the Glyncorrwg pilot would pick up the coaches and propel them to North Rhondda at 14.15, making two trips, the last of which would continue through to Cymer/Corrwg, leaving Glyncorrwg about 15.00, Nantewlaeth 15.05 and arriving Cymer/Corrwg 15.10 to make the connections. The engine would run round the train and return to Glyncorrwg empty coaching stock, when it would be run around again and the coaches would be placed in the carriage sidings overnight. (For a short period, around 1947 they also ran the night-shift colliers' train from Cymer/Corrwg to North Rhondda leaving Cymer/Corrwg about 22.20 arriving back at 23.10.) The Glyncorrwg train crew would be relieved at 16.00 by a crew from Duffryn Yard who had travelled to Cymer on the 14.52 from Aberavon Town. They would call into Cymer Afan booking office for a warrant to travel in the Western Welsh bus to Glyncorrwg. This crew would work trips of empties up to South Pit and North Rhondda, returning with a load until the collieries were clear of traffic, leaving Glyncorrwg at about 18.45 for Duffryn Yard with the outward traffic, putting the up-liners off at Cymer/Corrwg on the way down.

The Glyncorrwg porters would clean the station, issue tickets, deliver and collect any parcels, weigh the coal lorries for delivery of coal from the mileage sidings, take the numbers of the wagons from the collieries and enter them into the necessary books, clean out the coaches, maintain the Tilley lamps in the yard, the signal lamps, and load up any sheets and ropes etc.

With the closure of Tonmawr tunnel (1,109 yards long) in 1947, the Duffryn Yard trains were diverted via the Rhondda and Swansea Bay to Cymer where they would be crossed outside Cymer Afan down home signal, crossed back through the exchange sidings into Caerau tunnel, to be crossed back over the viaduct to Cymer/Corrwg. The result of this closure meant that the South Wales Mineral Railway was closed from West End siding, Abercregan to Tonmawr. The line from Cymer/Corrwg to West End was kept, so that the Cymer pilot could pick up the loaded coal from there. This track remained until a ramp had been built near the goods' shed at Cymer and the owners of West End had to load their coal into wagons from there. When the line to Tonmawr closed, the electric train staff instrument was taken from Tonmawr box to Cymer General box and later into Cymer new box. There was an intermediate staff instrument and telephone in the Cymer/Corrwg booking office. Later on, the electric train staff was replaced with an electric token instrument, the only difference was that instead of the intermediate instrument being in Cymer/Corrwg, it was repositioned in a hut over the other side of the viaduct, together with the placing of a new catch point. Up until then it was possible to cross a train from Cymer Tunnel ground frame and from Cymer/Corrwg onto the viaduct at the same time.

With the closure of Nantewlaith Colliery, 1949 (where everything had to be delivered by rail as there was no road access) and the introduction of more buses to take the colliers to work, the workmen's trains from Cymer/Corrwg ceased to run (*c.*1953).

Cwmafan Railway Station

With the closure of the Rhondda and Swansea Bay Railway from Aberavon Town to Cwmafan in 1963 and also Duffryn Yard later on, the goods' trains for Glyncorrwg started from Margam. They were diverted via the Llynfi Valley, via Cefn Junction and Tondu.

All the trains to North Rhondda would be propelled up from Glyncorrwg with the brake van leading, as there was no other means of getting the van behind the train on the way back with a load.

At South Pit, ground frame No.2, a spur had been constructed which acted as a trap and van siding. This spur was on a gradient opposite to the ruling gradient, which was 1 in 22, with the result that the brake van could be run back up the spur and wait there until the engine had gone by, when the van would be run down the spur, the catch point then set for main line and the van gravitated behind the engine, ready to pick up the coal at South Pit. (This occurred for trains from Glyncorrwg to South Pit only, when the van would be behind the train going up.) Before reversing the nearest runaway catch–point above Glyncorrwg signal box, South Pit outlet, the head shunter or guard would telephone the signalman for permission for the

Cwmafan Railway Station

Cwmafan level crossing

Nantawlaith brick factory

train to leave. The signalman would then leave the box in order to close crossing-gates (reputed to be the largest wooden-framed, at 30 feet 6 inches) on the western region across the road. The two wicket gates were operated from inside the box. Owing to the frequency of opening the gates and the shunting movements under the 'Marks' system, the signalmen were made up to class 3.

I was told by my father (who had also worked at Glyncorrwg) that at one time, around 1910, there was a police sergeant ('bobby') who would call to the station and borrow a tricycle that was kept there, put it on the rails and cycle to Cymer. I believe that this 'bobby' may have referred to the signalman as they were also called bobbies years ago.

About three-quarters of a mile below Glyncorrwg there was a Per Way cabin made of sleepers. One weekend around 1944, a large rock became dislodged after heavy rain and rolled from the top of the mountain down to the river, demolishing the dry-stone boundary walls and flattened the cabin. The South

Wales Mineral Railway had a dry-stone boundary wall each side of their railway line from Tonmawr tunnel to Glyncorrwg. (The other railways in the Afan Valley used wire fencing.) The building of these walls must have taken up considerable time and cost, owing to them being built on the mountainside.

Around 1955, when Zammit's demolition company were preparing a brick stack for demolition at Nantewlaeth, the vibration of the Cymer pilot travelling from Glyncorrwg to Cymer with a full load at about 13.15 caused the stack to fall across the railway line after the passage of the train. It then became necessary to open up pilot working to the point of obstruction until cleared about six hours later.

In 1946, a light engine, travelling from Tonmawr to Glyncorrwg at 09.35 hit a small baker's van travelling from Abercregan on Jarret's crossing, wrecking the van by squashing it against Cymer/Corrwg platform. The two occupants of the van got out without injury but the van was mangled.

During the blizzard and heavy snowfall of 1947, the 03.10 freight train from Duffryn Yard train with a banker load of empties for Glyncorrwg was forced to come to a standstill opposite some Abercregan houses. The fires of both locos had to be dropped and the train remained there for two days, during which time most of the coal had been taken from the locos and used in the houses!

About a quarter of a mile below the cutting, where the Nant-y-bar houses stood, there was a farm crossing leading from Rhiw Cregan Farm to Rhiw Cregan Hotel – also known at one time as the Prince Albert – but more commonly known as the 'War Office'. The reason for this nickname, I was told, was owing to the number of fights fought there between the local inhabitants and the sinkers of Duffryn Rhondda Colliery, when they were sinking the pit. By this crossing, on the Cymer side, can still be seen the remains of a stone platform. My wife's great-grandmother, Mrs Anne Davies, got off a train here on 12 August 1882 and on her way home she heard some children screaming down by the river. A young girl had fallen in. She jumped in the river and saved the child, but lost her own life in doing so. This information has been taken from her gravestone, a white Celtic cross, at Jerusalem cemetery, Pontrhydyfen. Whether there ever was an official passenger service on the Tonmawr to Cymer/Corrwg section of the South Wales Mineral Railway is debatable but I can remember my grandmother and many others telling me that during Neath Fair, the women of Glyncorrwg would sweep out the coal wagons, and wooden benches would be put in for them to travel in these wagons to the fair. What was the platform of the 'War Office' built for? Was it only to unload the beer? And how did my wife's great-grandmother get off a train there? I can remember the 06.10 Duffryn Yard being used, unofficially, to take the children from packers' houses (these were two railway houses built by the side of the track by Nant-y-bar stream, originally built for the Per Way men's families, hence the name packers) and the Nant-y-bar houses to Abercregan school and, when older, to Cymer Senior School. The 06.10 would stop at West End (incidentally, this colliery was worked by means of a double rope way where the weight of the loaded tram would pull the empties up the incline), to pick up loaded and put off empties. The loaded would be put off at Cymer/Corrwg. So the shunt suited the children from Nant-y-bar to Cymer and did not mean any extra stopping for the train, other than at packers' houses, where it would arrive around 08.15.

When anyone died at these houses (which were roughly opposite Duffryn Rhondda Post Office), owing to the road access being so poor with only a pathway by the side of the railway track – they would be unable to get the hearse down there. So arrangements would be made for the coffin to be placed on the Per Way trolley at the rising of the funeral, when it would be pushed to Abercregan or Jarrett's Crossing, Cymer where the coffin would be placed into the hearse to continue its way to the cemetery. The timing of putting this trolley onto the line would have to coincide between the time the Cymer Pilot would put the electric train staff in at Cymer/Corrwg at approximately 13.15 and 15.05, when the section would have to be clear for the colliers' train to run from Glyncorrwg to Cymer/Corrwg. The Glyncorrwg Per Way ganger, whose length started near Paddy's Bridge and ended at North Rhondda, would contact the signalman from Cymer/Corrwg intermediate staff instrument to ask for a staff to be released, for protection during this period when the trolley was on the line. I was told of one instance when the funeral was on the point of rising at the house and they were waiting for the arrival of the vicar/minister (I don't know what denomination). The weather was bad and there was no sign of him, so eventually the ganger said, "I can't wait any longer. I've got to replace this staff by 15.00." The poor man's lawyer, who was also there, said "Well, we can't leave the house without a short service. We'll ask Mr Jack Watts, next-door neighbour of the deceased [a railway signalman at Abergwynfi, also a lay preacher] to say a few words." He was only too glad to oblige. The coffin was then placed on the trolley and pushed to Cymer/Corrwg. When they arrived there, the vicar/minister was waiting in the hearse and he told the poor man's lawyer, "Sorry I couldn't make it to the house but the weather was too bad," to which the 'poor man's lawyer' replied, "As far as we are concerned, you can go back home because you are not being paid for today. We can manage without you. Have we got to look at the barometer to organise funerals these days?!"

The track from Abercregan West End to Tonmawr remained until *c.*1953, before being picked up. Packer's Houses were pulled down *c.*1965. The poor man's lawyer lived in Abercregan and received that nickname for the advice he would give to people making claims for compensation etc. and for the quickness of his wit.

Domestic water for packers' houses was had from the *pistyll* below the culvert under the South Wales Mineral Railway, until Rhiw Cregan Farm closed *c.*1945. The railway company then piped the water from the old farm supply – still from the stream – to the houses.

Water for the 'War Office' was had from a well near the pathway leading down to the river footbridge.

A short distance below the packers' houses can be seen a high wall of stone built at the side of the mountain. At one time there were sidings and a screen here, where wagons would be put off and picked up by the South Wales Mineral Railway. From here, there was a tramway on an incline to Nant-y-Bar Colliery. Further down the line, the remains of Paddy's Bridge, named after the Irish navvies who built it to maintain the right of way over the South Wales Mineral Railway from the bridleway running from Cynon football field to Nant-y-Bar Farm, can still be seen.

Roughly opposite Cynonville houses was a junction at one time, leading off the South Wales Mineral Railway to Pontrhydyfen. This was called the No.8 railway. I was told by one old railwayman that this line was only used once and then only by a ballast train. Why this was so, I don't know. In *The Story of Glamorgan* (1908) by C.J. Evans, there is a photograph on page 95 of what seems to be two signal posts near the junction. If this is so, No.8 railway was there prior to 1908. I am of the opinion that this railway was put in after the Port

Talbot Railway had approached the Rhondda and Swansea Bay Railway about a link up of their railways in anticipation of the extra coal traffic expected to come from the Tonmawr area. As the map of the Port Talbot Railway shows, there were collieries dotted all over the place here. It was supposed to be a place of great coal potential and with the planned building of new and bigger collieries, prior to the First World War, when the south Wales coal industry was at its peak, expectations were at their height. (I was told by one elderly person that German engineers were in the process of putting new and bigger winders in one of these collieries when war was declared, with the result being that these men were sent home and the winders were never put in.) With these expectations and also the number of collieries already served by the South Wales Mineral Railway section in the Afan Valley – West End, Nantewlaith, Ynys Corrwg, South Pit, North Rhondda and Crow's Nest – they could see the time was coming when Tonmawr would become a bottle neck, so the natural thing for the Port Talbot Railway to do was to divert any traffic it couldn't cope with, such as to and from the South Wales Mineral Railway in the Afan Valley, via the No.8 railway to Pontrhydyfen and the Rhondda and Swansea Bay Railway. The South Wales Mineral Railway had an outlet at Cymer but I am sure Cymer also would have been unable to cope with any extra traffic, owing to the amount already using the junction.

When the First World War was over, the extra coal traffic from Tonmawr didn't materialise and the south Wales coal industry went into decline, so the No.8 railway wasn't required as the Port Talbot Railway could cope on its own, with the result that all that remained of the No.8 were the points from the loop in Pontrhydyfen and approximately a quarter-of-a-mile of track, which was now used as a siding with a wheel stop, to prevent any traffic running back out of the siding. This was used until the 1950s to serve a small area on the mountainside known to the railwaymen as Potts's Colliery, named after the station master at Cwmafan at the time who I think, was a shareholder.

After the closure of Tonmawr tunnel, this siding was also used to cross the 06.10 Duffryn Yard to Glyncorrwg banker load, should it run late and be unable to get to Cymer before the passenger train was due, as it would be too long to get in the loop at Pontrhydyfen.

Tonmawr/Gyfylchi tunnel, which was 1,109 yards long, was partly lined in brick, the remainder being just bare rock. It was closed in 1947 owing to a landslide at Tonmawr end. I was told by one old platelayer – who had relaid the track in this tunnel in the 1930s and who had just read a book stating that the South Wales Mineral Railway had originally been broad gauge – that he couldn't believe it. "Do you know," he said, "we could just about manage to get standard gauge track in, as the tunnel was so narrow in places. And I remember them sending the colliers' coaches through there for Glyncorrwg, years ago, and all the handles were ripped off the coaches." After that, whenever it became necessary to change these coaches for some reason, they always went via Cymer viaduct.

I was also told in 1975, by a Mr Jones of Tonmawr, who had been a local councillor there and was the owner of a coal level at Abercregan and who at the time was 94 years old, that there had been a head-on collision between two locomotives in this tunnel (as previously mentioned). Both drivers, he said, were brothers. When I mentioned this incident to a loco driver, he said he had read an article about it in *The Lighted Flame* – a history of the Associated Society of Locomotive Engineers and Firemen.

Mr Emlyn Davies, a retired railway official who had been

through this tunnel on numerous occasions when he was a fireman, told me that the guards of the trains would sometimes take the side-lamps off the van before entering the tunnel; otherwise they were likely to be knocked off, owing to so little clearance.

Another person who would have been born around 1898 told me he could remember walking a tunnel in the Afan Valley as a young boy, which was lined with white bricks. I said "You must be mistaken," as there was no tunnel that I knew of in the valley lined with white bricks. When I asked the aforementioned plate-layer, he said, "Yes. There were white bricks in Tonmawr tunnel." I, myself walked through there in 1953 and I don't remember seeing any but, I wonder if when the Port Talbot Railway took over from the South Wales Mineral Railway or perhaps before, it became necessary for some reason to line with brick part of the tunnel which hadn't previously been done during the broad-gauge period, with the result that there would be limited clearance in these parts and a total lack of manholes. So, was there a possibility of either using light-coloured bricks or whitewashing as an indication of this limited clearance to the trainmen and anyone walking the tunnel? Should anyone be in the tunnel when a train approached, their only option for safety, apparently, was to lie down by the side of the track. Over the years, these light-coloured bricks or whitewash would have been covered with an accumulation of soot, smoke and dirt.

During the Second World War, the military stored an ammunition train for a number of weeks on the South Wales Mineral Railway between the level-crossing house at Crythan and Tonmawr. They had a number of men from the Royal Navy to guard it and there was a relief signalman there all the time, as a hand signalman to clip up onto points in case it became necessary to move the train at any time.

Cymer Railway Station with the Refreshment Rooms on the left

In the mid-1950s, when the National Coal Board decided to modernise South Pit, Glyncorrwg, there was quite a lot of coal coming out of the colliery and I can remember talking to Mr Fred Screech of Cymer who, at one time, was the man in charge of the weighbridge at Nantewlaith Colliery and was now one of the officials for transporting coal for the National Coal Board at Tondu and he said, "Do you know, John, when they have finished the new work at South Pit, the coal will be coming out like a waterfall and I can't see the railway [British Railways] being able to cope with it." Needless to say, less coal came out and the same can also be said about Duffryn Rhondda Colliery.

To get back to the normal day working at Cymer, the two signal boxes, Cymer Afan and General were interlocked by a lever we called the 'bolt' and each box had to have this release before they could make use of the exchange siding.

The 08.00 Aberavon to Cymer Afan freight train (the Cymer pilot) would arrive with any traffic for Cymer – Glyncorrwg/ Abergwynfi and Llynfi Valley, at about 09.00. These wagons would be put off and the Cymer foreman would have taken the tally of the yard and handed it to the shunter to say what shunts were required in the yard. On Thursdays, the beer van had to be taken over the Afan up-main so that beer could be unloaded for the Refreshment Rooms.

After the 10.00 Afan and General passenger trains had departed they would start shunting. A lot of this would be done at the General box by using the mainline No.1 (called the 'long siding') and the exchange sidings. This would be completed by 11.30 and the train formed with Glyncorrwg traffic. Anything for Nantewlaith would be put off on the way up. The engine would have water and the train would return to Cymer about 13.20, picking up at Nantewlaith if required and putting off at Cymer/Corrwg sidings. Then they would stand in the middle road (between the two boxes) awaiting relief of the trainmen, who would arrive at Cymer on the 14.00 from Aberavon. At 14.30 the light engine would leave for Duffryn Rhondda East. It would have been accepted under the warning, to pick up the two rear coaches off the 13.50 workmen's Treherbert to

Duffryn Rhondda Colliery which closed in 1966

Duffryn Rhondda Halt, which had left Cymer Afan at 14.15. These two coaches would then be crossed into the pit siding on the downside near to the colliery baths to wait. The 13.50 workmen's train would then run around and leave Duffryn Rhondda for Treherbert at 15.10. The next train leaving Duffryn, the 14.35 from Neath, would leave there at 15.20. The two-coach workmen's train would leave the pit sidings, cross to the up-main and would leave Duffryn at 15.30. Later on, it was retimed to leave there at 16.00 for Blaengwynfi, where the two coaches would be put off into the shed road, ready to be picked up by the next freight train. This was called B.G. and taken through to Treherbert for the following day's working. The Cymer pilot would take water and return to Cymer where they would pick up the brake van and empties for West End and clear out the loaded, go to Nantewlaith and pick up the loaded (the colliery had closed in 1949 but the screens were still handling coal from Glyncorrwg and the patent fuel plant remained open for a few more years). The up-line traffic would be put off at Cymer/Corrwg sidings ready to be picked up by the Tondu trains later on. The down-line traffic would be taken back, with the pilot leaving Cymer about 19.00 for Aberavon and Duffryn Yard, picking up at Duffryn Rhondda West if required.

Excursion trains from the Rhondda Valley to Porthcawl, up until the alteration of the layout of Cymer in 1960, would be brought to a stand at Cymer Afan down-home signal and the foreman would get on the engine and pilot the train through the yard via the exchange sidings and propel back outside Cymer General up home signal, after he had first made sure all the necessary points had been clipped and padlocked and all other movements in the yard were at a stand.

The longest passenger train I remember, passing Cymer,

was a school excursion from Neath to Bristol Zoo in 1946 or 1947, via the Rhondda Valley, picking up school children at different stations. It had thirteen coaches and was drawn by three locomotives (from Taff Vale Railway 0–6–2).

Owing to the heavy snowfall and blizzards of 1947, the rail traffic at Cymer was severely disrupted for about three days. I went to work on the first day at 06.00 and found that the previous night's 'Rodney' was still in the platform at Cymer General. Apparently, it had arrived three hours late and they were unable to run the engine owing to the snowdrifts. So, it was decided to get a light engine from Tondu to pick up the coaches and take them back. This engine was coupled up to the coaches and started to pull them back but the second coach became derailed, owing to the accumulation of snow in the points outside the signal box leading to the exchange siding. It was a good job the driver noticed it very quickly, otherwise the coach would have demolished the General signal box. The light engine returned to Tondu but the engine of the 'Rodney' and coaches remained there for the next day until the snow plough was run to Abergwynfi through the General loop and returned, after which the break-down arrived to rerail the coach. During this time, the trainmen made use of the General waiting room and lit the biggest coal fire in the grate there that I had ever seen, to keep warm. They had plenty of steam coal from the loco to keep it going.

On the Cymer Afan side, the first train to run that day was the 21.35 Neath to Pontypridd which arrived at Cymer Afan about twelve hours late and apparently the loco had to be filled up with water by means of a hosepipe from the National Colliery Board baths at Duffryn Rhondda.

Gradually, the drifts were cleared with the snowplough and Per Way staff. I was told that some of the miners also helped out so that they could get back home. After the line was cleared, the first trains to run were engines and vans with milk churns and bread for some of the villages. Not a lot of bread though, as most of the villages at that time had their own bake house.

Plans had apparently been drawn up in the 1930s to modernise Cymer Afan Station. The new signal box was to be built near the station master's house (now the site of the library) but these plans had been shelved owing to the depression and the Second World War, the idea being to do away with three signalmen's posts and having an island platform to do away with a booking clerk, two porters and a lad porter, together with the maintenance of some of the buildings. In the late 1950s they looked into the plans again and this time decided to build the new signal box a few yards further down from Cymer Afan Rhondda and Swansea Bay Railway box. This signal box and new layout was put into operation in June 1960. With this, the Hump Yard at Margam and the new modernising plans for Port Talbot General, together with the introduction of diesel multiple units – a little later – we were told that eventually they would be introducing a frequent circular passenger service to Cardiff General and back, via Bridgend, Cymer Afan, Treherbert and Cardiff Queen Street and another set from Cardiff General and back, via Cardiff Queen Street, Treherbert, Cymer Afan and Bridgend. Everyone was quite optimistic about the future. This feeling, however, did not last long.

Duffryn Rhondda Halt came under the supervision of the Cymer Afan station master. It was staffed by a checker, on duty from 08.00 to 16.00, or from 16.00 to finish. The day-shift shunter at Cymer would travel down there on the 06.15 colliers' train, open up and work there until the day-shift checker came on duty at 08.00, returning to Cymer on the 08.15.

On the down-platform was a building made of wood and corrugated sheets, incorporating a waiting room, booking office and a parcel office. The checker would meet the passenger trains, booking and collecting tickets. Parcel traffic for Cynonville would also be put off at Duffryn Halt. He would go around the colliery in the morning taking the tally of all loaded wagons received to work out the demurrage due if they were not unloaded on time; make out the daily and weekly wagon returns, phoning them in and also the numbers and destinations of all wagons to be forwarded, arranging for them to be picked up, together with what wagons were required for the following day. He performed the shunting duties when the Cymer shunter was not available, sometimes shunting until 01.30 on the late shift.

The checkers were regraded around 1956 when they were made up to working foremen. This was when a small colliery called Foel-y-Duffryn started working and loading their coal at the ramp by the mileage siding near the West box.

All the railway staff working at Duffryn were allowed a firewood block on blockdays (Tuesday and Thursday), the same concession as the colliers, but one new manager, around 1955, put a stop to this which only lasted for a few weeks when he realised that the cost of demurrage had increased and the various shunts the colliery required could not be performed! He was better off letting them have the blocks!

There were three class 4 signalmen to cover Duffryn Rhondda East and West boxes, the hours of duty being: 06.00 to 14.00, or from 14.00 to finish or 15.30 to 23.30. Each of the signal boxes was equipped with a switch to switch in or out of the circuit. The block section, when both boxes were switched out,

Duffryn Rhondda East

was Lower Cynon to Cymer Afan. The signalman coming on
duty at 06.00 would open up and switch on the East box, then
when required would switch out and open up the West box,
then close the West box return to the East box until relieved
there by the 14.00 to finish signalman, who would work there
until 15.30 when he would be relieved by the 15.30 to 23.30
man, who would work there for the full shift. The 14.00 to
finish man would walk down to West box, sometimes working
there to 02.30 until all the loaded traffic had been cleared out.
On the other hand, if the colliery was on strike, he could finish
about 17.00. At times, if there was a signalman short they would
be put on extended hours, both men working back and fro
between East and West.

The first Duffryn Rhondda East box was two storeys' high.

Later on, the coal owners of the old colliery had permission to build a bridge for their tramway across the Rhondda and Swansea Bay Railway to enable them to take across some of the coal and spoil to be dumped by the side of the river. This bridge was built right by the side of the signal box, with the result that the signalman's view was restricted. This box was burnt down about 1912 and the men working there at that time worked under tarpaulins until a new box was built. (I was told this c.1955 by Mr David Jones who had been a signalman there at the time.) When they built the new box made of wood, it was three storeys' high, to enable the men to see over the top of the bridge and have a better view of trains approaching from Cymer and the points and signals.

The stone buttress for this bridge could still be seen by the side of the box in 1965. I was nearly responsible for burning this box down again! I would go there to work, quite often as a relief signalman. This particular winter's morning in about 1956, I had difficulty in lighting the coal stove and I could see that the stove pipe was blocked, so I got some paraffin-soaked waste and put it in the pipe and ignited it through the trap door that was used normally to give access to a cleaning brush. The pipe started to roar and vibrate with sparks showering everywhere. Thank God things cooled down, but I never had trouble lighting the stove again! I wouldn't recommend this means of cleaning a stove pipe to anyone.

The old Duffryn Colliery was a slant dug under the main road to Cymer, on the bend about 50 yards passed the Powell Duffryn Office – now Baker's building stores – near the stream where the colliery had built a small dam as a feeder for the pit top. I was also told by my father, William J. Morgan, who worked in the new colliery in 1913, that at one time there was a wire rope across the river Afan from behind the East box to the houses in Nant-y-Bar, so that bags of coal could be pulled across the valley to supply the houses there, as there was no other way this could be achieved at the time.

Apart from shortening the double-line block section, Lower Cynon to Cymer Afan, the East box was required open for empties and inward loaded traffic to be put off for the old and new colliery. Also for the Treherbert to Duffryn Rhondda workmen's trains, which terminated and returned from there after the engine had run around. The box would normally be open from 06.00 to 23.30, Monday to Friday and 06.00 to 18.00 Saturdays only, apart from about 10.30 to 12.30 each morning/afternoon when the signalman was working the West box.

The points between the up-platform and signal box were

Duffryn Rhondda West

mostly used to put coal traffic off for the Glyncorrwg Urban District Council gasworks, which closed c.1958.

The old colliery outlet siding by the National Coal Board baths was last used to cross the two-coach colliers' train to wait time.

Up-trains of empties from Aberavon would pull up clear of the top siding points, brakes would be applied and the brake van cut off and run back clear of the siding points. The empties would then be propelled into the siding, the brake van gravitated back to the signal box and the engine crossed to the down main via the top cross-over to the down-platform; the down cross-over would be reversed and the brake van gravitated on to the engine. When this had been completed, the van and engine would be propelled back on the down main to the signal box to wait for the signalman to switch the East box out and accompany the engine and van to the West box and switch in to pick up any outward traffic. The engine and van would have been signalled under the 2–2–3 train-stopping-in-section bell signal, to Lower Cynon.

When the engine and van had arrived at the West box, the signalman would switch into circuit and then cancel the train-stopping-in-section bell signal. One advantage of this box was that it had electric light. It was the only box in the Rhondda and Swansea Bay Railway section in the Afan Valley to have electricity, until Cymer new box was built in 1960. All other signal boxes in the Afan Valley were lit either by gas or Tilley lamps. Not one of the East or West boxes or the Halt had a toilet or running water. The men had to rely on the colliery baths. The West box had been built to allow coal traffic to be picked up from either the pit or washery sidings of the new colliery. The pit sidings were mostly used for large and cobbles from the screens, coal that had been washed being picked up from the other sidings. There was also a mileage siding on the down side, near the signal box where coal from Foel-y-Duffryn was loaded and any other local traffic was left there to be unloaded.

Blaengwynfi East signal box came under the supervision of the Cymer Afan station master. It would be open from 05.45 on Mondays until about 03.00 Sunday mornings after the passage of the Landore to Pontypridd parcels' train. The bottom of the box was built of dressed stone and the top of timber at the end of the down-platform. It had about thirty levers, was a single-line crossing station, with water columns for the locos and at one time, controlled the inlet and outlet of traffic for the tunnel colliery (which was near the old Blaengwynfi police station) and Scatton Colliery (which was opposite the Graig council houses) and Blaengwynfi West box. This box was taken out of use in 1945, its points to and from the loops then being worked by motor points generated by hand from the East box which had a shed road. The last time this siding was used was to stable the two coaches of the colliers' train that the Cymer pilot had worked from Duffryn Rhondda Halt to Blaengwynfi. They would be standing there from 16.20 until about 18.20, Monday to Friday, when the next up freight train, the Blaengwynfi goods train, would pick them up and take them to Treherbert for the following day.

Blaengwynfi East

The Rhondda tunnel between Blaengwynfi and Blaencwm was just a chain short of two miles long and during the time of steam, the distant signal for each box was, more often then not, obliterated with smoke. So the drivers could not see it, even though they had built a ventilation shaft near the Blaengwynfi end of it. To overcome this problem the Great Western Railway

Blaengwynfi East

had placed a gong, incorporating a wagon buffer that had been placed upside down by the side of the track at the distant signal and a plunger placed by the inside of the rail, so that when the flange of each wheel passed over it hitting the plunger, the gong would resound. It was a very effective system – especially for young lovers, warning them they had only about a quarter of a mile of darkness left before reaching the home signal and daylight!

The signalman had also been instructed to fill up and light a Tilley lamp and place it on its post opposite the down starting signal during the hours of darkness, to enable the goods' guards to apply the hand brakes on the wagons at the Stop board.

The signalman would help the porter to collect the tickets of the last train from the Rhondda on a Saturday night owing to the large number of people leaving the train. It was quite an interesting place to work with plenty of activity and people coming and going, but one big disadvantage was someone or other would quite often miss the last train through to the other valley and as it was a long trek by road over the mountain would take the risk of walking the tunnel.

Blaencwm signal box

Lower Cynon signal box controlled the end of the single-line section from Pontrhydyfen and the start of the double-line block section to Cymer Afan (or Duffryn Rhondda West/East if they were switched into circuit). It came under the supervision of the Cwmafan station master. It had an up-refuge siding which was also one of the spring points for anything running back from the up-main. This siding was rarely used as most up-freight trains had been crossed into Pontrhydyfen loop to give preference for up-passenger trains. At one time, the box also controlled traffic to and from a small coal mine by the side of Nant Cynon.

The box was made of wood apart from the chimney breast which was bricked. After the closure of Tonmawr tunnel in 1947, when Duffryn Yard to Glyncorrwg trains were diverted via the Rhondda and Swansea Bay Railway section, the box was opened from 03.10 Monday until after the clearance of the Landore to Pontypridd parcel train about 02.20 Sunday morning.

Pontrhydyfen signal box controlled a single-line crossing station (token to Cwmafan and token to Lower Cynon). It also came under the supervision of the Cwmafan station master. It opened at 03.00 Mondays until after the clearance of the Landore parcel/milk to Pontypridd at about 02.20 on Sunday mornings. It had a goods' loop, a goods' shed and siding and another siding for Rhyd Avon Colliery, plus a single line that had been built to join up with the South Wales Mineral Railway – which was called No.8. The box was made of wood and stood on the

Blaencwm signal box

embankment at the end of the down-platform and was lit first by oil, then Tilley lamp. There was a water column on each platform. The water for these and the station toilets was piped from a small stream about a quarter of a mile towards Lower Cynon and was stored in two big tanks. It was not suitable for drinking, however. Drinking water had to be collected and carried each day from a stream in the wall of the siding for Rhyd Avon Colliery – a distance of about 100 yards from the box.

The station buildings were comprised of a booking office, waiting room, gents' and ladies' toilets all under one roof and built of dressed stone. (In years to come this could have been converted into a beautiful bungalow!) This was the last building on the Rhondda and Swansea Bay Railway – apart from the Refreshment Rooms at Cymer Afan – to be built to this standard. On the up-platform stood a small wooden shelter and the whole of the premises was lit by oil lamps, apart from the final year when Tilley lamps were used. The platform porters were withdrawn about 1950, after which they put repeat block bells and a telephone in the booking office, allowing the signalman to leave the box and book tickets for any passengers. For doing this extra duty, the morning signalman was paid 30 minutes of extra overtime each day for making up the books and sending the cash to Cwmafan. The cleaning of the station and lighting of the platform lamps was carried out by the Cwmafan shunter.

Pontrhydyfen Station

There was a head-on collision on the single line between Pontrhydyfen and Cwmafan about a quarter of a mile below the rock at about 17.40 on 25 November 1960 between an up-diesel multiple unit and a down-freight train (which were due to cross each other at Pontrhydyfen) with the result that the driver of the diesel multiple unit and the fireman of the freight train were killed and four seriously injured plus a number of sustained injuries. The Ministry of Transport inspector, Col. D. McMullen's report was published on 13 April 1961.

Over the years the signal box there had subsided quite a few degrees so they were going to rectify this and had already dug a trench that was to be filled with concrete so that the box could be jacked up a week later. Arrangements were made to have the necessary hand signalman available for this operation when the Swansea's assistant superintendent came up to have a look at the scene. His comment was it was not necessary, and for the

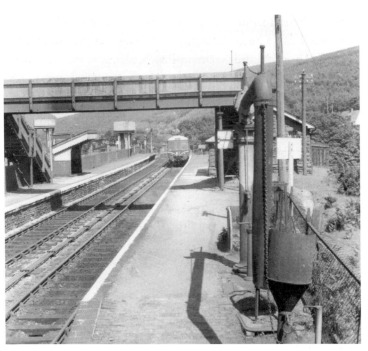

Pontrhydyfen Station

signal box and the station to be closed. The box was closed the following week. Instead he altered the timing of some of the passenger trains that were timed to cross at Pontrhydyfen by about ten minutes and they then crossed at Cwmafan. But there was a drawback to this plan. The railway company had to give a few weeks' notice to the public when withdrawing a service, so to get around this they berthed a brake third coach on the up main by the platform so that the signalman on duty could advise any passengers and book the tickets from there. They had already clipped up the points and taken off the signal arms and had the single-line section worked by token from Cwmafan to Lower Cynon and that was the end of Pontrhydyfen station!

But the first railway station in the Afan Valley to close was Cynonville. Both platforms can still be seen. It had a waiting room and a booking office built of wood that stood at the top of the steps that led down to the down-platform – situated just before the stone bridge. This building was demolished about 1942 when the station became unstaffed. The platforms were gas-lit and the guard of the 16.30 school train to Aberavon would turn them on in the wintertime when he arrived and the guard of the 23.20 to Cymer would turn them off. Later on they were worked by a time switch.

Above the station and about 20 yards before the old chapel, stood at one time two small brick-built army billets and toilet facilities for a small searchlight unit. These were built at the start of the Second World War and remained there until about 1947. The searchlight itself had been positioned in what is now the car park of Afan Argoed Country Park.

In 1960 when the Conservatives were in government and Mr Ernest Marples was Minister for Transport (who was very, very pro-motorway and anti-railway) he decided to stop any more rail investment and appointed Dr Richard Beeching – a scientist and director of I.C.I. to become chairman of British Rail. He was told to "make the railways pay". His full report came out in 1963 but, in the summer of 1962, there was talk of the passenger service on the Rhondda and Swansea Bay Railway coming to an end. I had been booked to open Aberavon seaside box for a week, for the excursion trains from the Rhondda and Glynneath Valleys. These trains were full, so we were quite optimistic and thought they would never do it, as we had also heard from some of the railway officials at this time, that with the alteration of the layout at Port Talbot General Station and the new panel box, the intention was for the Rhondda and Swansea Bay diesel multiple units to pull into the General,

Pontrhydyfen signal box

the driver would change ends and pull out to Briton Ferry via
Aberavon Seaside and do the same on its return to the Rhondda
and Swansea Bay Railway. But this never happened! The
passenger service from Briton Ferry to Cymer Afan finished
after the last train on Saturday, 3 December 1962. Detonators
were – unofficially – placed on the track to mark the occasion.
The link to the Rhondda Valley for passengers remained, with
a service from Bridgend to Treherbert worked by the Tondu
trainmen.

Around about this time, Mr Idris Owen, who had been on

the railway since 1930 and had been working in the Per Way department but now, owing to ill health was a leading porter at Blaengwynfi, had gone to London for a few days' holiday and while on Paddington Station, he happened to meet an old railwayman called Benjy who, at one time, had worked as a clerk at Cymer Station. He asked Idris where he was currently working with Idris replying Blaengwynfi, to which Benjy said, "If you take my tip you'll get from there as soon as you can because that's not going to last long!" Benjy must have had some idea of the plans for the future as he was now working in the main office of the Western region.

With the withdrawal of the passenger service from Cymer Afan to Briton Ferry, it meant leaving only the output from four collieries to be catered for: Tonmawr, Duffryn Rhondda, South Pit and Avon, plus two small mines – Foel-y-Duffryn and West End. So the Rhondda and Swansea Bay section was, more or less, left intact for about two years, at which point they decided to close the line from Cwmafan to Briton Ferry and, at the same time, closed Lower Cynon signal box, clipping up the points and picking up the up-main from there to Duffryn Rhondda West but leaving the down–main as a single line to Cwmafan, closing that signal box and now leaving it as a ground-frame to run around coal trains to and from Tonmawr.

The steam locos and trainmen would now come from Treherbert and not Duffryn Yard, as before. Trains for Tonmawr would leave Duffryn Rhondda West, go to Cwmafan, run around, then back to Tonmawr via the Oakwood ground-frame, likewise on the way back to Duffryn West. Trains from Duffryn Rhondda and Avon Collieries were also worked by steam locos.

The Glyncorrwg pilot for South Pit was diesel hauled and worked by Margam trainmen, who came via Tondu. This all seemed to work well, the main thing being that the link from the Afan Valley to the Rhondda remained open for the passenger service.

With the closure of the colliery at Tonmawr about 1964, there was now no necessity for the single line from Duffryn Rhondda West to Cwmafan and the line from Oakwood ground-frame to Tonmawr. Duffryn Rhondda also closed in November 1966 but the washery there remained open until January 1970 as they continued washing the coal from Avon Colliery. This coal was picked up from the Avon by the Cymer pilot, taken down to Duffryn where it was sorted out and washed, then brought back to Cymer for the Merry-Go-Round trains to pick up for Aberthaw Power Station.

Duffryn Rhondda East and West boxes had been closed and the line to Duffryn was now classed as a siding, with run-around facilities and a stop-block positioned down by the junior school and roughly opposite to where the West down-advanced starter had been. Points to put empties off or loaded at the old East and points to pick up outward traffic at the West were now converted to hand-points.

Around 1968, a train fully loaded with coal, hauled by a class 37 left Cymer with a brake van at the rear. On arrival at Duffryn, they cut off the diesel to run around the train, which was then pulled back to above the entrance to the top-siding, near to where the East up-advance starter had been. But, somehow or other, coupling near the brake van broke and most of the wagons ran back about a mile until they hit the stop-block, the gradient being about one in 79. No-one was injured.

The next thing we heard was that the Blaenrhondda tunnel had to close, following the inspection in February 1968 by the chief civil engineer of Western region, as he considered it to be unsafe for passenger trains. I went to work Cymer signal box on a Friday night to find a notice that stated the tunnel was to close after the last train on the following day. So, when my mate, Cyril Mitchel, gave me 5–5–5 on the bell to indicate he was opening Blaenycwm box on this Saturday morning, I phoned him up and told him "Do you know Cyril – that is the last time you will ever do that?" "What do you mean?" he replied. He had heard nothing. But that box did remain open for a short while after this. The last train through this tunnel was an officer special with the general manager and other officials, also Mr Sidney Green, the National Union of Railwaymen General Secretary. The train did not stop in the tunnel as it travelled through the block section at the same speed as a normal passenger train took. I do not remember the actual date of this but I do remember the chief signalling inspector of Cardiff division, Mr D. Jones, coming up to Cymer box and telling me, "This train will stop here for half an hour," as they were going over to the Refreshment Rooms for a drink. "Sorry you can't come over, signalman, as you are on duty!" I thought to myself you could put a pint over the bar for me though as I would be finished at 14.00. What a hope!

We were still optimistic that the tunnel would be reopened, as the Minister of Transport, Mrs Barbara Castle had refused to withdraw the service. It had also been said, in 1962, that the link of the Afan to the Rhondda Valleys should remain open, as an alternative bus service over the mountain road could not be maintained throughout the year. The bus service was put into operation, temporarily at first. The passenger trains would now run from Bridgend to Cymer, where the passengers would transfer to the bus for Blaengwynfi and Treorchy and back.

A joint staff consultation meeting under the chairmanship of Mr F. Paterson, the assistant divisional manager, was held at Cardiff on Tuesday, 6 February 1969, for the withdrawal of the railway passenger service from Bridgend to Treherbert. The management and staff put forward their cases but the result was that the chairman regretted that the staff representatives were obviously not convinced of the management's explanation and that the proposals could not be implemented until the Minister of Transport had received the report after the public meeting had been held of the Transport Users Consultative Committee for Wales and Monmouthshire at: 22, The Chambers, 68, St Mary Street, Cardiff. CF1 1FD, the secretary being Mr E.G. Gomm M.B.E.

Treherbert Railway Trade Union's Joint Action Committee had printed and distributed, on 21 April 1969, an appeal to all organisations and interested parties to drum up support to save the Treherbert to Bridgend railway passenger service, stating their case and ending with:

> Please help us by discussing the enquiry at every opportunity and creating, thereby, interest which will lead to the filling of the Town Hall, Maesteg on Thursday, 15 May, at 10.45, giving maximum support to the local authorities in presenting their case of hardship to the Trades Union Congress.
>
> Yours sincerely,
>
> T.V. Lewis and E. Evans (Joint Secretaries)
> Gordon Coles (Chairman)

When the day of the Trades Union Congress meeting arrived, there were quite a lot of people in the town hall but by no means was it full. I would say about a third full and the people that had objected were called up to voice their reasons and their case for the service to be retained. I would like to point out here that the bus service to and from the Llynfi Valley to the Afan Valley at this time was excellent and no way could the railway have improved on this. Most of the travelling public would use this service, i.e. the first bus from Cymer to Maesteg was 05.55 and then every half-hour until 22.55, and Maesteg to Cymer 06.15 and the last one at 23.15, Monday to Saturday, run by the United Welsh Bus Company. So, as far as the majority of the travelling public from the villages to their local town Maesteg were concerned, they would not be greatly affected with the withdrawal of the trains, apart from mothers with prams or suitcases, etc. The main difficulty would be for anyone who had to travel from the Rhondda.

The next thing to close in the Afan Valley was Avon Colliery, which closed in September 1969.

The new Minister of Transport (Mrs Barbara Castle had been appointed to a new position in the government), gave his verdict about the closure after receiving the Trades Union Congress report and gave his permission to close the tunnel and withdraw the passenger service in May 1970, after which British Railways Western Region advised the public that the service would cease after the last train on 20 June 1970 but the school train would run until the end of term on Thursday, 15 July.

This was the end of the rail service in the Afan Valley and the passenger service in the Llynfi Valley, but the coal industry there remained intact with Caerau, Coegnant, St John's and Maesteg washery still working. (But their time for closure was soon to come.) The general opinion locally was that the very thought of closing the Blaenrhondda tunnel – the shortest distance between quite populated valleys and usable throughout all seasons – was a very retrograde step, in fact, sheer madness!

All that remained now was to close the stations, and Cymer signal box. The latter was dismantled and rebuilt as a new signal box at Bargoed Station. All staff involved with the closure were made redundant. The Per Way department had picked up and loaded onto bogie-bolsters some of the points, fittings and rails to be used on other layouts on the Western region. These wagons were picked up by the last train in the Afan Valley. It arrived, engine and van, on Saturday, 22 May 1971, diesel number 6994, 1,750 h.p. English Electric, from Margam. The driver's name was D. Keen, second man E.L. Smith and the guard I. Stenner – known as 'Sahib' as he had spent time in the army in India! This train left Cymer at 10.50 and I took a few photographs of it as a record. When you look at them, note the number of houses with smoke rising from the chimneys due to coal fires.

I also took photographs of the last passenger train from Cymer at about 22.20 on 20 June 1970. People may think how was it still light enough at that time? Because that was the year that they tried double-summer-time, as they had done during the war.

The track and station buildings that remained were sold to a demolition firm as scrap. The first sounds to be heard when this gang of workers began pulling up the track were the keys being knocked out of the chairs that held the rails and a metallic clang of steel against steel, echoing across the valley when the sledges and bars hit the rails, finishing off forever now, what had at one time been called the 'permanent' way. It was a sound I hated as this railway had played such a big part throughout my life and my father's before me. It had always been kept up to a high standard, its buildings, the Per Way, fences, drains and culverts routinely checked. Ben Edwards, a ganger, had even received a certificate for the 'Prize Length'. If anyone deposited rubbish onto railway property to get rid of it – as it seems common-place to do today – the gangers made sure that those responsible removed it! If the ganger

The last booked passenger train W55023 Cymer–Bridgend, 20 June 1970

didn't notice it, the Per Way inspector who walked the length regularly would want to know why it had been overlooked. If the inspector missed it, the chief engineer would remark on it when he passed through on his inspection train maybe about once a year.

When the demolition gang had finished their work, the only features of the railway to remain were its track beds (now used as cycle tracks or footpaths) the stone-built seven-arch viaduct (which has been seriously vandalised), the stone pillars and ironwork of the viaduct that led to the South Wales Mineral Railway Gelli tunnel, a few stone over-bridges and, last but not least, the Rhondda and Swansea Bay Refreshment Rooms,

Diesel No.6994 – last train in the valley, 1971

where you can still call for a meal and a drink, situated on the old up-platform which are more-or-less intact and serve as a reminder of the heydays of the railways in Cymer.

Now that I had been made redundant I had to make a decision – what was I going to do? I had been working on the railway for 25 years, counting my two years National Service. Should I look for a job outside the railway industry? I couldn't drive at the time, so I decided to apply for the signalman's post at Gelli Las, which meant that my bus fares would be paid for and I would retain my rate of pay as a district relief signalman. I then took my wife's advice and started driving lessons as we could see that owning a car was fast becoming a necessity. I began

Neath & Brecon signal box

work there in May 1973. It was a single-line crossing station between Tondu Middle and Maesteg South boxes. It could be switched out when not required. It had a 43-lever frame and electric token instruments to both boxes. Soon after I started work there, Caerau, Maesteg North and Maesteg South were closed and the single-line section was then to Llynfi Junction and the box could no longer be switched out. About 1974 they also closed Llynfi Junction box and put in a no-signalman's token instrument for that section. Gelli Las had been built about 1942, the same time as Llynfi coal-fired power station was built, its purpose to control the traffic in and out of there, together with the traffic in and out of the paper mill. I remained there until March 1978 when it closed, which was about two years after the power station closed. I was hoping to stay there until retirement, as there were supposed to be big plans on the cards for converting the power station into an incinerator which

June 1996: After 50 years of service on the railway, pulling the signals for the last time at Neath and Brecon signal box

would dispose of rubbish from the whole of Glamorgan and which would be brought in by rail. Alas, the best-laid plans of mice and men, it came to nothing and I had to move on again, this time to Tondu Ogmore Junction.

This box was quite a nice box to work. At one time it must have been a very busy place. Before I arrived there some of the layout had been taken out and the lever frame reduced by half. It was open for the three shifts but closed on the weekends. It was double-line block to Tondu Middle, O.E.S. key working for the Garw branch, telephone and message working for the single line to Caedu signal box on the Ogmore branch and O.E.S. key working for the Werntarw branch. I remained working there until it closed in 1983, when I picked up my bags again and went to work at Neath and Brecon Junction.

This box was a fringe box for Port Talbot panel multiple aspect signalling. It had telephone and ticket working on the Neath and Brecon single-line to Blaenant and O.E.S. key on the single-line Vale of Neath branch to Aberpergwm. I stayed there for twelve years until my retirement in July 1996, thereby completing over 50 years employment on the railway, 99 per cent of which I can honestly say I thoroughly enjoyed.

Postscript

One of the most optimistic things I heard around 1988 was that they were thinking of bringing back the passenger service in the Llynfi Valley to Maesteg. Apparently, 'those that be' only wanted to reopen Pencoed and Pontyclun (Llantrisant) stations but the local MP, Peter Walker, had the foresight to tell them that if they wanted this, they would have to reinstate the passenger service all the way to Maesteg. The track was still down but the coal industry there had been run down – the same as had happened in the Afan Valley, years previously. (It's a sin that they picked up the track there so quickly – to be sold off as scrap – otherwise, that too could have been reopened.) After all the cuts and closures of pits and railways in the whole area, it was good to hear of something positive happening at last. The passenger service to Maesteg was finally reopened in October 1990 and has since proved to be very popular and well patronised.

Foundation stone of RSBR tunnel – length 3,443 yards. Opened in July 1890.

Cymer Afan Station

Cymer
Corrwg

Duffryn No.2,
Duffryn Yard

Duffryn Rhondda West

Duffryn Rhondda East

Caerau Station

Caerau signal box

Blaengwynfi Station
© Gareth Tilt

Pontrhydyfen Station

Tondu Ogmore signal box

Nantyfyllon signal box

Llynfi Junction signal box

Blaencwm

Blaencwm signal box

Maesteg South signal box

Llynfi Junction signal box

Last train on the Port Talbot railway line, 1964

Incline at Briton Ferry

RHONDDA
AND
Swansea Bay Railway.

CHEAP
MARKET TICKETS.

COMMENCING JAN. 1st,

Market Tickets will be issued at

CYMER FOR ABERAVON

Every SATURDAY, and by any TRAIN.

FARE:

TO-AND-FRO, THIRD CLASS,
ONE SHILLING.

Passengers holding these Tickets will be allowed to carry, Free of Charge, the same weight of Luggage as Passengers holding Ordinary Tickets.

These Tickets are available on the day of issue only.

BY ORDER.

Aberavon, December, 1885.

Llewellyn Griffiths, Printer, &c., Pelly-street, Cwmavon.

Poster for cheap tickets

4

Anecdotes from the Railways

S OME OF THE following stories took place before I started work on the railway. They were related to me by my father, William John Morgan, signalman, who started his railway career in 1927 at Cymer.

Dai 'Treorchy', signalman c.1936

He would go up to the goods' shed and pick up a handful of Indian corn from one of the sacks that used to be delivered from the shed to the local shops. He would then go outside the General signal box and lay a trail of corn from the points outside the box, across the lines to the backs of Margam Street, then go back to the box and wait for the chickens to find the corn. When one approached the points, Dai would be waiting with his hands on the lever and, quick as lightning, the points for No.1 siding would be over and Dai would have a chicken dinner ready for his family! He had also placed nest boxes in the rail weighbridge that was in the loop line opposite Cymer General box and with the aid of another trail of corn, had tempted the hens to lay there.

When the onion sellers from Brittany came off the train, Dai would welcome one of the regulars back saying how glad he was to see him, "Let's go over the Refresh for a pint." After about five minutes, Dai would say, "I'd better go back to the box to see if the train has cleared the section. I'll be back in two minutes." While the onion seller was talking to the other men in the pub, Dai would be stocking up with onions. During the war, the onion sellers were unable to come over. After the war was over and on his first trip back to Cymer, the first thing the onion seller said as he got off the train was, "Where's bad lad Dai?"

Dai also started to run a few raffles to stretch his income, but it didn't last long as once it was discovered that it was always someone from Treorchy who was winning the prizes, never anyone from this side of the Rhondda tunnel!

He was due to go and see the superintendent at Swansea High Street to be disciplined, as he had caused a derailment at Cymer Goods shed. A van had gone over the stop block and landed on the platform. The superintendent and the district inspector were waiting for Dai to turn up, but to no avail. The district inspector, Mr D. John, went to Cymer General box the following morning to find out why Dai had failed to turn up. His reply was, "To be honest, Mr John, I'm sorry but I haven't got a pair of shoes to wear, only these daps you see on my feet and I was too embarrassed to travel to Swansea like this. I can only just afford to buy shoes for my family!"

"What size do you take, David?" Mr John sent him a pair of shoes so that Dai could go and see the 'super' to have a ticking off. (I would like to point out that this was in 1930 when there was no social security or family allowance.)

If ever Dai was on the train with a few of his mates and there was no room for them all in the same compartment, Dai would sit down and keep scratching himself until some of the other passengers got up to change compartments! If he was told someone was without coal, he would always help out by jumping on the wagons and helping himself. (I have also done this, as I would know the policeman on duty and say that so-and-so has no coal. "I'll be back for a cup of tea in half an hour," he'd say!

Dai 'Treorchy' was so-called because his surname was Jones. This being a very common name in the area, nicknames were given to differentiate between them, some examples of which follow: Dai 'Potato', named after a well-known sea-captain who ran the blockade during the Spanish Civil War; Dai 'Half-pint' because he was so small; Dai 'Fat' because he was overweight – but not as much as some are today; Dai 'Carmarthen' and Dai 'Glasgow' which are self explanatory and last, but not least, Dai 'Lucky' as he had happened to mention one day how lucky he had been not to be labelled with a nickname! There was also a Dai 'Stick-a-fork' and a Dai 'Piece-of cord', but I don't know why!

The Rentman

A new relief porter came to learn the job at Blaengwynfi. Jim, one of the signalmen there at the time, and was full of life and fun to work with, soon discovered that the new recruit was a bit slow on the uptake and decided to pull his leg a bit. He asked the porter "Have you been told about the rent collecting?" "No," said the porter. "What rent?" Jim handed him a railway notebook on which was written some names and addresses of people he knew (and who were in on the joke) together with the amounts of 'rent' due opposite their names. "Rent on railway houses – you collect it every Friday," said Jim. Friday came and the porter set off on his rounds. At every house he received the same reply, "I'm sorry, I can't pay this week. I'll double-up next week!" When the porter got back to the station, he told Jim, "I've had a gutsful! I've done 'em all and no-one has paid!" Jim said, "You need to be more firm with them boy, otherwise they'll take you for a ride!"

Blaengwynfi *Echo* boys

I had not been to Blaengwynfi box on relief for months. Then I was told to go and relieve the porter there. After booking the 18.00 up- and down-passenger trains, I would go up to the signal box to have a chat with my mate Jim, the signalman on duty there. I knew the *Echo* boys would be there sorting out the papers for delivery. When I walked in, I could see they were new boys and didn't know me, so I put on the most official voice I could muster and said to Jim, "You know, signalman, that the signal box is private. Get these boys out straight away." "Sorry, Mr Morgan," said Jim, "the only reason they are here is to sort the papers out in case the wind blows the *Echo*s away. And they give me one free paper each evening." "Fair enough," I said. "They can have just ten minutes each night if there are no trains around." I then left and went up to the booking office, during which time the boys asked Jim who was I and he answered that normally I worked Paddington's departures signal box but that the box was so busy there that they had to send me back to Blaengwynfi every four months for a rest. "It's all right though, boys, he'll cool down in a few days!"

The following night I asked the boys how much they were getting paid per week for delivering the papers. "Ten shillings [50p]," they said. I told them that if they were doing the same job in London they would be getting £2.10s. (£2.50p) per week. "How's that?" they said. Jim was quick off the mark and said because they had joined the *Echo* boys' union and that if they joined, they too, would be entitled to £2.10s., plus a bicycle, wet weather clothing and a duffel coat! "How do we join this union, then?" "Don't worry," said I. "I know the union secretary Mr Hammond very well and will get him to send some forms down for you when I go back to work up in London." I warned them not to tell the newsagent about it until they had signed the forms, in case he would give them the sack! To save time Jim said that we had better measure them up for their duffel coats. We did, with a wooden foot ruler! The following month I was working afternoons at Duffryn Rhondda signal box when Jim got through to me on the telephone after first phoning my father (who was in on this prank) at Cymer Afan signal box and saying, "Didcot, would you put me through to Paddington departures box please?" A short pause, then, "Hallo John, the *Echo* boys would like a word with you." The first thing they asked me was had I seen Mr Hammond yet? "Yes," I said and that he would send the forms down in a day or two. They also asked how much a week would the contributions be, and I said 3d. but that Mr Hammond had said they would not have to pay for the first month as they were the first to join from the Afan Valley! I asked my uncle, who was the National Union of Railwaymen secretary for our area, for a few forms for me. Jim cut off the National Union of Railwaymen on the top of the forms and went up to the booking office to stamp them with the rubber stamp for CHILD and BLAENGWYNFI to make them look official. The boys signed, thinking they had now reached 'El Dorado'! Now, the repercussions were to come! What about the duffel coat and bike? What would the newsagent have to say? What would the boys' parents have to say? Jim had some solutions. "I've got a new railway fogman's coat with a red collar they can have, instead of the duffel coat!" So he packed it up and sent it to one of the boys c/o Blaengwynfi Station. The boy tried it on and Jim said he looked like Father Christmas, as it was much too big for him. "John must have given the wrong measurements," said Jim. "I'll measure you again." The newsagent came down to the station and asked what the hell we were up to, as the boys had asked him for £2.10s. a week and a bike! "Otherwise they'll report me to some Mr Bloody Hammond!"

I was in Blaengwynfi signal box a few weeks later when one of the *Echo* boys came down to the station with his mother to catch a train over to the Rhondda. I thought that's bug★★★★d it! I've got to go on the platform to change the tokens. When the boy saw me he said, "Mam, that's the man who told me about the union!" Now for it! But she took it in good spirits and we both had a good laugh.

Another trick we pulled with them was to keep the previous night's copy of the *Echo* clean until the following evening. Then, when the boys weren't looking we would put last night's paper into the front and back sheets of the following morning's and wait to see the result of an angry customer receiving stale news! (While on the subject of the *Echo*, in the 1950s a railway management meeting had been called to discuss improvements, as there was a shortage of applicants for jobs. It turned out to be a load of bullshit. One of the workers got to his feet in disgust and stated, "When I applied for a job on the railway I had to produce two reputable testimonials. Now, you can get in with a bloody copy of the *Football Echo*!")

No doubt playing practical jokes like this is now taboo but to people of my age – 78 – putting up with pranks was part of growing up. All my mates and I had run the gauntlet when we were young. It did more good than harm. The *Echo* boys ended up with better jobs than Jim or I. One joined the police force and did well, another became an electrician and my wife and I met the third a good few years later in Cardiff. He came up to me and said, "John! It's great to see you! Do you remember when I was young? You and Jim told me I was destined to go places? Well, I've been!" I heard that he had joined the Merchant Navy but his next bit of news I hadn't heard. "I married an Australian sheep-farmer's daughter and I'm back in Wales for a few weeks."

The Earwigger

One signalman on the Port Talbot Railway in Bryn box spent quite a lot of time on the telephone. He would sit down with the handset in his hand, listening to all the conversations on the box-to-box telephone. One of the other signalmen told the signal and telegraph technician about it. "I'll cure him!" he said. The following week he took an old telephone up to the box and put it in place of the other one. He also placed it on the wall so that the signalman had to stand up to speak into the mouth piece and hold the ear piece to his ear at the same time to carry on a conversation!

Trespassers in the Rhondda tunnel

As mentioned previously, I used to enjoy working at Blaengwynfi. (Abergwynfi only came under us during its last six months, previously being relieved by the Cardiff division.) It was easy to get to and I had some good mates there. But at one time, I began to dread the night shift between 23.40 and 01.00, Monday/Friday and 22.45 and 01.00 Saturdays only, when the last train to Blaenrhondda would have gone. I'd hear footsteps coming up to the box, then a knock on the door and someone or other would ask the same question, "Any chance of a lift on a goods' train through the tunnel, signalman?" So normally, I would make enquiries and if there wasn't I would light the fogman's hand lamp, give it to the person and tell him how much time he had to walk through – which would take about 50 minutes – and for him to be sure to hand in the lamp at the next signal box, Blaencwm, about two miles away. The signalman there would phone me on receipt of the lamp and I'd know the trespasser was out of the tunnel before the Landore to Pontypridd parcels' train was due to go through.

This used to work well until one Saturday night when a middle-aged man called up and asked the usual question. I can still see his bloody face now, after more than 50 years! I said, "Make sure you hand in that lamp to my mate in the next box so that I will know you are through." But he didn't! With the result that after waiting for nearly an hour, I began to worry that he had fallen or been taken ill. I was due to close the box for the weekend after the up-parcels train and I would have to fill out a 'Please Explain' form if I stopped this train. So I told my mate at the other end, "I'm going to walk through to check and make sure." He said he would walk in part of the way, too. I lit the Tilley lamp and, as I didn't have a watch, put the brass clock (three and a half inches in diameter) from the signal box in my pocket and set out. I walked three-quarters of the way through and met my mate. We had found the tunnel empty. I said to him "That's the last b★★★★★d I ever give a lamp to!" Sweating pints, I turned on my heel and walked back to Blaengwynfi box, just in time to accept the parcels' train. The person did hand the lamp back – more than a week later! But I was not on duty and never saw him again. How could I have gone home, wondering if there was someone lying injured in the tunnel and in possession of a fogman's oil lamp, to boot! The only answer to my problem was to fork out for a cheap torch and hope that it would be returned by the borrower. The only alternative to this easy, short walk (in the dry and with a light of some sort) from the Afan to the Rhondda Valley was a six-mile walk by the side of the unlit A 4107 main Bwlch-y-Clawdd road to Treorchy, an uphill climb to 1,700 feet, then downhill and not a house or any other place of shelter for miles. There was very little traffic using this road at night in the 1950s, so any chance of a lift was negligible.

Another tunnel incident

I remember this happening about 1958. It could have been quite serious but, if it had to happen, it could not have been at a better time. The up Aberavon to Blaengwynfi workmen's train had passed through the Gelli tunnel at 14.30 and the sub ganger, Mr Will Lloyd, started to walk the length of the tunnel after it. The tunnel was only 169 yards long but you could not see through from one end to the other as it included a bend. As he walked he noticed a chunk of the crown of the rail had come off. Knowing the next one was the down Pontypridd to Swansea passenger train, due to pass at about 14.50, he ran and put down detonators to protect the line.

I had been relieving the grade 1 porter at Blaengwynfi on the day shift, and had finished and was going home to Cymer on that down-train. Hearing the sound of the three detonators exploding and the train coming to a stop, I got off the train and saw the guard and Will Lloyd who told me what was wrong. I said I'd go back to Blaengwnfi to inform the signalman and ganger. I walked to the main road and was lucky to get a lift back immediately. The ganger and his men put the Per Way trolley on the line, lit the trolley lamps and we were back at the site in no time. I thought, how are they going to solve this? His answer was to put down a chair key – a piece of hard wood, about six inches of three by three – in place of the broken crown, then call the driver of the passenger to run over it very cautiously. Once the train had gone by, they took the Per Way trolley to Cymer and picked up a rail to replace the damaged one. During this time a bus was put on in lieu of the train between Cymer and Blaengwynfi.

Place your bets etc.

When relieving a signalman at Cymer Afan box in the 1950s, I noticed that the locker I was using had a narrow slit cut out at the top of the wooden door, just enough for a letter to be slotted in. Being inquisitive, I asked one of the workers the reason for this. His reply was, "A few years ago, one of the previous signalmen was a bookie's runner and whoever wanted to place a bet would put the details in an envelope and post it there if he was not on duty at the time!"

Another signalman was a self-taught, brilliant sign writer for any organisation that required one: rugby clubs, cinemas, drama weeks at the workmen's hall etc. Most of his work was for the local cinema, called The Cosy. He would also make slides to be shown on the screen advertising the forthcoming attractions. Once a year, the slide would wish 'A Merry Christmas and a Happy New Year to all our Patrons', decorated with holly leaves and berries.

One signalman also acted as the cellar man for Miss Davies, the landlady of the Refreshment Rooms who was getting on in years. He was also one of the village's special constables and had received their long-service award.

In the Cymer General box, one signalman repaired clocks and watches for local people and was also secretary of the Great Western Railway St John Ambulance class, held at the station. There were about eight of us and we all got an extra free ticket providing we passed the exam each year, which was taken by the local doctor, Dr J. Taylor.

Another signalman's hobby was his big glasshouse, where he grew beautiful flowers, tomatoes, cucumbers etc. to sell at reasonable prices.

Yet another signalman was the local barber. No time was wasted if you wanted a short back and sides – you just popped up the box for five minutes, had a cup of tea and waited for a gap in the trains.

One of the gangers, W. Edwards, asked me one day if I could help him to finish off a coffin he had made out of seven by one floorboards, for the family of his friend. It was for a stillborn baby, whose mother was heartbroken. My job was to sandpaper it down and put on a cross, made out of veneer, on the lid. I was in the process of doing this when the chief inspector called unexpectedly. He had come by car, not by train, as they used to do. But he was very understanding. Shaking his head, he remarked, "I've seen it all now!"

There was quite a good working relationship between signalmen and officials in those days when work was work and camaraderie flourished. Some of the officials themselves had started off as signalmen. During my last few years however, all this seemed to change and not for the better.

The Tunnel Ghost

We had a new lampman about 1953 whose job it was to maintain and refill all the signal lamps from Aberavon to Blaengwynfi. The last lamp in his section was a quarter of a mile inside the

Blaenrhondda tunnel. He was about 25 years of age. The day he was due to do the lamps at Blaengwynfi, he called up to the signal box for the key to the oil shed to fill his cans up. Jim, the signalman, asked him how he liked the work. "Not bad at all," he said. "It's day shift regular. It suits me. I've got every night off, I'm single and I can go out with my mates. The only thing I don't like about it is walking this tunnel once a week." "How is that then?" asked Jim. "Oh, I don't like the dark!" That was enough to set Jim's mind working on a prank of some sort. "Why don't you walk through with Ben the ganger when he walks the length?" Jim suggested. (The ganger would walk the length every day in those days.) "Then you would only have to do the walk back by yourself." "That's a good idea," said the lampman. "I'll go down and see him for you now," said Jim, helpful as ever!

When Ben and the lampman were in the tunnel, Ben mentioned the 'ghost' that was supposed to haunt the tunnel. "What ghost?" said the lampman nervously. "Oh, it's a load of bull," said Ben. "Someone got killed in here, years ago, and every now and then his ghost is said to appear but I've been walking the tunnel for years and I've never seen it." Then, after a short pause, he added, "But some of my gang have!" sowing the seeds for the poor lampman's next visit to the tunnel. When the two of them arrived at the distant signal, they parted company – Ben walking through to Blaenycwm and the lampman returning to Blaengwynfi. As he entered the signal box, Jim asked him how it went. "OK," he said. "It was nice to have company to walk one way. The only thing is, Ben mentioned something about a ghost." "Ah," said Jim. "I didn't like to tell you myself, as not to worry you, but take no notice of it." The following week, the lampman came to Blaengwynfi box and asked where Ben the ganger was. The signalman told him that Ben had had to leave early to walk the length. Downcast, the lampman said "Oh, I was hoping to walk it with him." The trap had been set!

Ben was waiting in one of the manholes about 100 yards from the mouth of the tunnel, ready and waiting with a lookout-man's horn in his hand. The lampman lit the Tilley lamp in the box and asked the signalman if there were any trains due. "No, you've plenty of time," he said. Ben, on the lookout, could see him coming closer and just as the lampman came past the manhole, he blew a mighty blast on the horn! The lampman let out a scream, dropping his oilcan and breaking the Tilley lamp and made a dash back to Blaengwynfi box. "That's the last bloody time I'm going in there!" he said. Henceforth, Ben the ganger did the lamp for him each week when he walked the length!

Shrinkage

The previous lampman, over 60 years old, was very small and, owing to his age, he had begun to stoop a little. He was one of the most conscientious men I have ever known. Just thinking of him now makes me realise just how easy some men earn their money. It was his job to make sure all the signal lamps in his district, from Aberavon to Blaengwynfi, remained lit. He would come to each signal box once a week on the day appointed and clean, trim and fill all the signal lamps for that box and they were always spotless, as was the oil shed where he would have his food. He would climb the signal posts to replace these lamps, irrespective of the weather, be it a gale, a downpour or a snowfall and you could rely on Fred to always call on the day appointed. All this for a low rate of pay. These lamps would last for eight days. Should one of them go out beforehand, there was a special form at each signal box to be filled in by the signalman and Fred would have to give an explanation, but I cannot recall any of my mates having to complete one of these forms, such was his standard.

When Fred called at Blaengwynfi box one day for the key to the oil shed, Jim was on duty for the first time. He saw that Fred could just about reach the key on the notice board, so he decided to move the nail holding the oil shed key a fraction higher up the notice board every three weeks, when he'd be on the day shift. Over the weeks, Fred had to stretch further and further, then stand on tiptoe and finally have to ask Jim to please get the key for him. "I didn't realise how small I'm getting. It's only a few weeks ago that I could reach the key easily, with both feet on the floor!

The Rabbit

One of Blaengwynfi's Per Way gang asked Jim if he knew anyone who bred rabbits, as he wanted one as a pet for his son. Jim said he knew someone who travelled to and from the Rhondda who had some, and would get in touch with him. The Per Way man gave him ten shillings (50p) with the understanding that the rabbit would be sent over by train in a day or two with one of the colliers. Every day, when the man came to work, he would ask, "Has the rabbit come Jim?" to which the reply was always, "No, mate. You've been caught there all right!" Jim got a cardboard box, cut small holes in it, attached a 'Livestock' label to it and addressed it to the Per Way man. The following morning the man asked as usual, "Has the rabbit arrived yet Jim?" The reply was, "Yes. It's up in the parcel office." "Good," said the Per Way man, "my son keeps asking me all the time 'When is my rabbit going to come?'." They both walked up to the office. "Sign by here," said Jim, handing him a form. Then he pointed to where the cardboard box lay. "There's no bloody rabbit in here, Jim!" "Well," said Jim, "there was one in there when I put the box in the office. I hope it's not one of those homing rabbits! It must have got out of the box somehow and made its way home through the Rhondda tunnel! There's nothing you can do about it now, as you've signed the book for it. You could try and make a claim form out to British Railways, but I don't think they'll pay up!" "Will you make the form out for me Jim?" "Oh, OK then!"

> Dear Sir,
>
> I would like to make a claim for the loss of one rabbit. Value: Ten shillings. Sex: Buck. Colour: Black and white. Age: About three months. It is apparent that the rabbit had urinated, and the box had disintegrated.
>
> Yours sincerely....

The rabbit did eventually arrive for the Per Way man's son.

Threat of Murder

There was a porter working at Blaengwynfi in the late 1940s who had been through a very hard time during the Second World War. He had been a prisoner of war for four years and subsequently suffered with bad nerves. All the staff were aware of this but found that in all other aspects that he was a perfect gentleman. One day, during 1947, something happened to upset him and, as a result, he quarrelled with the station master and his temper flared. He grabbed the station master by the throat, saying, "I've had a gutsful of you!" Seeing a train come into view, he forced his victim to the edge of the platform and bent him backwards with the words, "I'll push you under this bloody train!" The station master, cool, calm and collected, replied,

"You do that G– and your cards will be up on the next one!"
An understatement if ever there was one! The porter pulled him
back. "Sorry, Mr Jones," he said.

To do with Fires

When a new signalman would start work in one of the boxes,
the other signalmen in the area would set a prank when the
cold weather arrived. One of them would phone up the
newcomer, pretending to be the chimney sweep on his rounds.
He'd instruct the new signalman to let his fire go out, as his
box was the next on the list. This left the poor man shivering
for a few hours in the early morning until 'the penny dropped'
or someone tipped him off.

During the Second World War the station master at Cymer
made out a roster of his staff for fire watching, as the station
was closed from 03.00 on Sunday until 05.30 on Monday.
Those on duty for this purpose would use the porters' cabin
as their base. One night, during these hours, the wagon repair
shed – about 200 yards away from the cabin – caught fire and
burned to the ground. This wasn't discovered until daylight the
following morning. That must have taken some explaining!

The government advised all industries to train their
employees ready for fire fighting. The Great Western
Railway had supplied stirrup pumps to each station and a
smoke bomb for this training. The station master at Cymer
made arrangements to have as many of his men as possible
to assemble outside the air-raid shelter which had been built
at the side of Cymer General signal box. Then he'd go and
light a smoke bomb inside the air-raid shelter and his men
would take it in turns to enter with a hosepipe from the stirrup
pump and try to put the smoke bomb out as soon as possible.
Everything was going to plan, with each man courageously

doing his best, until the signalman on duty at the General box – Bill Jones – decided to make the exercise a little more realistic. He fixed a detonator (fog signal) to the handle of the fire poker and dropped the poker, detonator first, onto a flat stone between the signal box and the air-raid shelter. There was one almighty explosion and a stampede from the air-raid shelter to safety. The station master advised his staff to keep well away from the shelter until the following day, when he would go inside, collect the remains of the smoke bomb and send it back to Swindon for analysis, as there must have been something wrong with the bomb! Before this could happen, Bill thought he had better own up, otherwise there would have been an official enquiry!

Pigeon Traffic

Each station in the valley used to get a lot of pigeon traffic during the training season as there were a lot of pigeon fanciers in the valley. They would bring their baskets down to the station for them to be weighed to work out the costs and then put them on the train. When the pigeons arrived at their destination, the porter there would open the basket and liberate the birds. Then he would write the time of liberation on the label and send the empty basket back to the station from whence it came, for collection. The owner of the birds would then time them coming back to the loft and would be able to work out how fast they had flown home. I can remember one fancier from the Graig Houses, Abergwynfi (about three-quarters of a mile from the station) coming to Blaengwynfi station and paying for his pigeons to be sent to Treherbert – a short flight to start them off for the training season. He told Idwal, the porter, "Don't forget to put them on the up 10.00 train for me, as I'm working afternoons and I want to be up in the loft when they come back. The next train will be too late." "Don't worry, I'll make sure they are on the train," said Idwal.

The 10.00 train came in, he collected the tickets, started talking to someone, gave right-away to the guard – and the train went out. The pigeon basket was still on the platform. Idwal, quick-thinking, used his initiative! He carried the basket to the tunnel mouth, liberated the birds there and put the time the train was due to arrive at Treherbert on the label. But he forgot to allow time for the birds to get their bearings to fly home from Treherbert. Once airborne, the birds could see their loft. When the owner called for the basket the following morning, Idwal, trying to sound casual, asked how the birds had done. "If they keep this up," said the man, "I'll win all the races. I've never had such birds!"

Family Matters

If one of the signalmen mentioned on the omnibus telephone (box-to-box) that his wife was expecting a baby, all his mates would soon get to know about it and soon the expectant father would be showered with gifts for the baby: dresses, booties, toys, prams and pushchairs etc. The only trouble was they were all second-hand.

I went to relieve one box and, as I went up the stairs, I noticed a pram parked beneath them. I asked my mate what it was doing there. He said, "John, there's been one hell of a row here this morning! Do you know B– in the gang?" I nodded. "Well, his wife brought their baby down for him to look after, so that she could go to Maesteg, shopping. The baby is down the cabin now. I have been looking after it since 10.00. The ganger is doing his nut! They wanted to know if you would look after it when you relieved me, until the mother comes home. But I told them you didn't know much about babies yet, as you've only just got married and they couldn't expect you to take the responsibility of a three-month-old child." I fell for the story, hook, line and sinker!

When the next down-train came in and I went out to change the tokens, the driver asked me, "What's that pram doing under the steps?" So, I related the full story to him, adding, "The baby's in the cabin by the up distant signal now." The driver, with a look of concern on his face, said "That's not right. I'm going to report this to the N.S.P.C.C.!" When the train left me, I heard the driver blow his whistle a number of times as he approached the cabin. I thought to myself, I've done it now, I've dropped one there, I shouldn't have told the driver and wished I hadn't! The gang were due to finish in an hour and all would have been well with the baby home safe again.

When the gang finished, I sat in the box watching them walk back up the line and all I could see them carrying were picks and shovels. No sign of a baby anywhere! One of the boys shouted up to the box, "John? I'll take the pram home now!" But he walked straight past it with a beaming smile on his face and I knew I'd been had and that they were all in on it, including the driver!

Another mate discovered his wife was pregnant when they were both middle-aged. Both their other children had grown up and were 'out of the way'. "John," he told me, "when you get to my age and you see Phyllosan tablets – the ones that fortify the over-40s – advertised, don't be tempted. Leave the buggers on the shelf!"

A Miracle

One railway guard at Glyncorrwg had spent most of his shift unofficially loading up manure from the local colliery. He made sure he had a full lorry load. When he finished work he had to unload the lorry, with the result that he had been sweating streams for most of the day and ending up with bronchitis and being off sick for a number of weeks. When his mate, Glyn, heard that he was ill, he decided to visit him and deliver his pay for him. The guard's wife answered his knock. "How is Tom, Mrs–?" "He's very ill, Glyn, not at all well. He's got to stay in bed. It's going to take a long time for him to get over this." "Is it all right if I go up and see him?" She nodded, reluctantly. "So long as you don't stay too long to tire him." Glyn entered the bedroom and asked "How are you feeling mate?" The answer was some sort of a grunt and then silence. Glyn took Tom's pay packet out of his pocket and handed it to him. "I've brought your pay for you. There's extra this week because you worked your rest day."

Glyn told me afterwards that as soon as he mentioned 'rest day' John, like Lazarus rising from the dead, made a grab for the envelope. Tom hadn't told his wife about the extra money for working his rest day!

Something for Nothing

When I was a lad porter at Cymer, one of my jobs was to go up to Nantewlaith Halt and issue tickets to the colliers who were travelling back to Cymer on the 15.10 workmen's train which was composed of very old stock. I would travel back in the guards' van, which was also rigged out with wooden seats for the colliers. One of the young colliers, who always aimed for a seat in the van, regularly asked the guard for a cigarette as soon as he entered. When we got to Cymer, the guard told me, "He's always cadging my cigarettes and I'm fed up with it. I'll bloody cure him tomorrow. He'll never ask me for one again!"

The following day Tom, the guard, had a cigarette especially made and ready for the cadger. It was made of dried horse manure, a few soft hairs from a sweeping brush and a little tobacco. When the collier lit up and inhaled, he very nearly turned green. He smoked his own cigarettes in the van from then on!

Measuring for a Uniform

When a new lad started work his first thought was always how long will I have to wait for my uniform. Bill the signalman, reading through the notices, found there was a chief engineer's inspection train the following morning, so he told the new lad porter, "There's an inspection train out tomorrow, Dave." "What's that then, Bill?" Bill saw his chance! "Oh, they come round now and again to measure all the new entrants for their uniforms. The train doesn't stop. They take a photograph and use a theodolite as the train goes by. I'll let you know when it's due and tell you what you have to do!" The following day, Bill went out onto the platform with the Abergwynfi single-line token for the inspection train. He told the lad porter to stand to attention until the train got close to the signal box. Then, he was to hold his right arm in the air, turn around and touch his shoes with both hands, then touch his head and shout out his name and age. The engineer could not believe his eyes as this all took place as the train passed! On the way back from Abergwynfi, the engineer stopped the train by the signal box and said, "Excuse me, signalman. What the hell was wrong with that boy we saw on the platform on the way up?" "Oh, him," said the signalman. "He's hoping to have a job in your department!"

Threats

Just after the Second World War, there was a very strict, particular and conscientious new station master at Cymer, who was always making sure his staff came and went off duty on time and that they carried out their duties as per duty sheet. This was about the time when a few new recruits had just been demobbed. The station master would walk around the station and ask, "Where's so-and-so?" "Down the yard taking numbers, Mr J–." Soon afterwards, the porter would be seen walking down the road or perhaps coming out of the Refreshment Rooms and he'd be given a telling off. "The next time I find you away from the station or coming out of the Refresh, I'll send you to Swansea!" This went on for a time until one of the boys wrote an anonymous letter to the station master and had one of his mates, a guard, take the letter over the Rhondda and have it put on a passenger train from there to Cymer, thereby covering its source. The letter went something like this:

> You are spending so much time keeping your eye on your staff, when perhaps it would pay you to keep an eye on your wife! Have you ever noticed how much time she spends in so-and-so's shop? I'd keep both eyes on her if I was you!

Of course the station master did his best to find out who the sender of these lies was, but never did!

Cader Idris

The Rhondda and Swansea Bay Sick Benefit Society

President: J.B. Philps. Committee: E. Jones, W. Benjafield, M.L. Watls, J.Bruton, B. Cockwell, R. Laite, W.L. Daniels, J. Chambalain. Financial Secretary: F.L. Catalja, Pont Velindra, Port Talbot. Auditors: W. Johnson and E. Le Garrec.

I joined the above society as soon as I could as, for a few pence a week, it entitled me to about £1 a week if I was on the sick and had a doctor's paper. We had no other sick pay then apart for the National Health scheme, which came into force in 1948. Sick pay for signalmen came into force about 1965.

I also joined a football pontoon club of the Rhondda and Swansea Bay Railway section. Each member would pick a team out at random and the number of goals scored each week by that team would be added up over the season. The first team to reach 21 goals would win a small prize and the pontoon would start again the following week. The profit from this club would come to help pay for our annual bus trip which took place one Sunday during the summer, when we'd hire a Neath and Cardiff Luxury Coach to take us across the border to visit different places in England – the main reason being that the pubs there were open on a Sunday, but not in Wales!

The trip that sticks out in my mind was the one to Cader Idris (but coming home via England). Why we decided on this destination, I do not know. Before we started off it was raining. And kept on raining – for hours. You could see next to nothing out of the windows on the bus. I had never seen such a dark, dismal and depressing place in my life. Slate was everywhere. Slate tips, houses and roofs made of slate, walls and fences made of slate, slate everywhere you looked. And we never saw the top of Cader Idris, it was shrouded in mist and drizzle. I was thinking I'd have been better off spending the day in bed, as my shift on the following day began at 03.00. Being a relief signalman, I received my orders on a Thursday afternoon from the Port Talbot district inspector and I had been booked for 'extended hours' at Pontrhydyfen for the whole of the following week, working from 03.00 to 18.00 on the Monday and 06.00 to 18.00 for the rest of the week.

We didn't stay long at Cader Idris! We headed for England, where the weather was good and stopped at Knighton, called at a few out-of-the-way pubs and had a good time. During our pub crawl I remember one of the local train drivers – who was due to retire shortly – buying a pint for everyone of us saying, "I want to buy you all a drink in appreciation of the friendship throughout my working life. And if I don't buy you one now, I'll find it difficult to do so out of my old age pension. You can all buy me one back then!"

I arrived back home about 01.00 on the Monday morning. It was pointless going to bed, I thought, as I'd have to get up again in an hour and might sleep late. So I changed into my uniform had my sandwiches cut and jumped on my bike to cycle about five miles to the box. I hoped to have an hour's kip there at some point before finishing at 18.00.

The trip to Cader Idris put me off going to north Wales for years afterward, thanks to that trip, the weather and the slate. But I must say that I have since been to the area and its surrounds several times and have thoroughly enjoyed each holiday there. Travelling by train and car throughout the region, I discovered superb scenery that would take a lot of beating.

Shylock

Around 1940 one of the gangers at Cymer had a reputation for being as tight as a crab's arse. Another member of the gang decided to have a bit of fun over this. On his way home he hit a six-inch nail through an old penny and into a wooden sleeper. When the miserly ganger walked the length the following day and spotted the penny, he walked back to the cabin to get a pinch bar to recover the coin with!

When I was a signalman at Duffryn Rhondda I would have to work the East and West signal boxes. When walking back from the West box, I'd find some silver paper from a discarded cigarette packet, wrap it around an old penny to make it look like a half-crown and place it about five yards from where the driver of a train would stop on the up-platform. Then I'd go back to the East box and wait for the next up-passenger train. The driver would notice the 'half-crown' and get out of his cab to pick it up.

Arthur

Whenever I see a film of the First World War, I think of Arthur. I always remember my father telling me that he had met Arthur coming off the train at Cymer Station on his way home straight from the front Lline in France. His uniform was covered in mud and he also had lice on his body. My father asked him how he was and his reply was, "Will, I have been through hell." Arthur was the sub-ganger in the Cymer General Per Way gang. He lived for his home, his church (St John's) and his work. He would never leave anyone down and working with him was fun from start to finish. Prior to working on the railway, he had worked in the colliery. I remember him working in the gang until he retired at 65 but, after a few weeks, the railway company asked him if he would like to come back as a crossing-keeper at Duffryn Rhondda East and he was the first one they had there.

Arthur was a good storyteller. He once told me that, when he was working at Glenavon Colliery around 1910, he had a new boy start with him. He told the boy to fetch some candles for him – they used candles and carbide lamps in the level as this was house coal and they didn't need safety lamps. "Now, before you finish your work," Arthur said to the boy, "cut a shelf in the side of the coalface to put the candles on, otherwise the rats will eat them." This the boy did. The following day, Arthur was in work before him and nibbled at the candles. When the boy collected them, he said, "Arth, the rats have been at them!" At the end of that shift, Arthur told him to wrap an old coat around them before replacing them on the shelf – they should be safe enough like that. The next morning, Arthur was in early again. He took out the candles, nibbled them and rewrapped them. When the boy came in, he said, "The rats have had 'em again, Arth!" "Right," said Arthur. "When you come in tomorrow, bring a tin in for them. The rats will never have them in there." The tin was brought in and put on the shelf with the candles inside. The next day, Arthur, early again, took out the candles, nibbled them and replaced them. When the boy opened the tin, he was gobsmacked. He shouted to Arthur. "Those bloody rats get everywhere! If I stick them up my arse they'll find 'em"!

When Arthur started as a crossing-keeper at Duffryn Rhondda East, the National Coal Board and British Railways came to an agreement that the National Coal Board would put a cabin with a coal stove and seat in it, for the crossing-keeper. The first few weeks after the crossing was opened, all that was there was a corrugated-sheet shed, four feet six inches by four feet six inches by six feet high with no door. So Arthur would spend most of his time up in the East signal box, as he did for more or less the rest of his time spent working there. But as soon as we heard on the telephone that the district inspector was on the train (the signalman in the previous box would see the district inspector getting on the train and would phone up the next signal box and so on;

later on, they had their own transport) Arthur would leave the box, return to his cabin and light a wood fire outside and sit on a wooden sleeper by the side of it, looking forlorn as the district inspector passed. "When I get back to the office Arthur," he'd say, "I'll phone up the colliery manager and get them to put a stove in for you. I'm not having this!" A few days afterwards, the National Coal Board did put a stove in. I had never seen such a big one – we had a much smaller one in the signal box! So Arthur would light this stove, then come up to the box to cool off!

When Arthur finished at the crossing, we had a new crossing-keeper, an ex-signalman who had failed the eye test. In winter when there was snow about, I would report to Cymer Station (the workmen's train had been withdrawn) to help clean the points and disconnect them when required. Then I would walk to Duffryn, perished by now from the cold. When I got there, the new keeper would say, "You going up to a cold box, John? It's nice and warm here now!" Even though he had a key to the signal box, the thought of lighting the fire there for the signalman never occurred to him, despite everything being readily on hand. After a few days of his gloating I'd had enough. One day, he couldn't get to work owing to the buses not running, so the carriage and wagon boy and I took the opportunity to fill his stove pipe up with hard snowballs. This was on a Friday. On the Monday, he came to work and tried to light his fire. I had forgotten about our escapade until I noticed clouds of smoke emitting from under the corrugated roof of the cabin – it had no other exit as the pipe was still blocked with frozen snowballs. It took the crossing-keeper hours to get his fire going that day!

A Long Wait

One of the gangers, Mr Jim D–, had a little smallholding by the side of the railway line, where he kept chickens. One of the Swansea Bay loco drivers noticed them one day as he was passing. When he saw Jim next, he said, "You've got some nice chickens there, Jim." "Aye," said Jim. "What I'm looking for now are some Plymouth Rocks." "My mate breeds them," said the driver. "Well, do me a favour," said Jim "and ask him if he will sell me a sitting of eggs. I've got a broody hen in the cot."

A few days later the driver turned up with the sitting of eggs but, as Jim was out walking the length of the platform at the time, he gave them to I–, one of the gang, to keep for him. But I– was full of tricks. He took the eggs into the Per Way cabin, put some water in a bucket and boiled them on the fire there for a few minutes, cooled them and gave them to Jim when he returned. Jim put them under his broody hen and waited. And waited. So did the poor old hen. When Jim saw the driver next, he told him, "Do you know, I never had one damn chick out of that sitting!" "I'll get you some more," said the driver.

Cootie Coots

For anyone who doesn't know what a cootie coot is, I had better describe one. It is a fictitious animal, crossed between a bird and a ferret, only found near the railway at Cymer Afan, Duffryn Rhondda and one other place in mid Wales.

When a boy would start work repairing wagons at Duffryn, we would all tell him to keep an eye out for the cootie coots. "What are they?" he'd ask. So, we'd describe them and tell him he'd find them in the stone wall opposite Duffryn East signal box. When he came up to the box, he would sit staring at the wall in the hope of spotting one. If he should glance away for a second, we would shout, "There's one! Did you see that, then? Coming out of that hole there, look!" "No!" "They are so damn quick, you have a hell of a job to spot them. You have to keep your eye on the wall the whole time." "What do they eat, then?" asked the boy. "They catch birds as they fly past the wall." The afternoon signalman would come to relieve me and he would ask the boy "Have you seen any cootie coots today?" He would say no and I would say yes, so the afternoon signalman would tell him to bring in some bird seed, as they loved that and put it outside a hole in the stone wall. "But make sure you wear some heavy duty gloves to handle the seed, otherwise they'll have your hands off!" The boy would bring in the seed and we would accompany him to the wall, wait for him to set it down, then walk back to the box to watch and wait for the cootie coots to appear. When the boy had gone to oil the wagons, one of us would go down and remove the bird seed. We would keep this going for days, until the boy gave up and lost interest.

When outside contractors were pulling down the remains of Cymer General signal box and the old air-raid shelter and levelling off the ground in 1966, the railway look-out man, who was from Maesteg, came up to the box prior to them starting, to say what they intended to do. I said "Whatever you do, Harold, don't go near the old signal box." "Why?" he said. "Because there's a nest of cootie coots there!" "What the hell are they?" So I gave him a description. "Don't talk so bloody wet!" he said. "Harold, you have been warned. They go for the throat! The only thing they are afraid of is fire. It's only a few days since we had a few men down here with half a dozen terriers. Do you know, they killed three of the dogs and the others ran off!" "Well, I've never heard of them," said Harold. "Ah, that's because they only live in Cymer, Duffryn and mid Wales." When the contractors started work, Harold told them about the cootie coots but made sure he always stood well away from the 'nest' area!

Another young lad starting work on wagon repairs was told after a few days that the boy who was doing his job before him was so weak that he couldn't pick himself up in that coal scuttle. We'd always catch one! "Oh, I can do that!" We would empty the scuttle, get him to stand in it and watch him having a go. When he failed, we'd suggest he try a sack as that would be lighter!

Free Beer

I was working Caerau signal box in 1969. One afternoon, about ten minutes after the school train had left for Cymer and all the school children had left the platform, I noticed four boys walking away from the tunnel. I thought, now what have they been up to? Have they put something on the line? They can't have been up to much good.

So I took a walk up the line to investigate. Looking around I couldn't see anything amiss for a while, but then I noticed that where the contractors had pulled down the old Per Way cabin near the tunnel, having tidied up the area afterwards with grass clodges, that one or two of them had been moved. I pulled the disturbed clodges to one side and, lo and behold, what did I find? To my surprise and great delight: twelve half-pint bottles of beer! Not being greedy, I decided to claim just four of them – under the laws of treasure-trove. To be honest, I did consider taking the lot but thought, on reflection, that it would be more fun to limit it to four. When the boys who had put them there returned for their booty, they would be bound to accuse each other of the theft, as they would jump to the conclusion that anyone else finding them would have stolen the whole caboodle!

I had a few chuckles picturing the outcome – and the beer was good too!

The Fish Head

From 1940 until about 1946/47 there were women porters working on Cymer Station (and also on Blaengwynfi and Glyncorrwg stations) owing to the man shortage during the Second World War. One of the signalmen decided, naturally, to play a trick on them. The porters' cabin was on the Rhondda and Swansea Bay Railway down-platform, between the waiting rooms and signal box. There used to be quite a lot of fish being freighted by train to Cymer for Mr Jack Petty's rounds, and also to be transferred to Cymer General for the Llynfi Valley. Jack Petty would cut the heads of the fish off at the pick-up point. So, one of the signalmen collared a fish head and nailed it under the table in the porters' cabin. When the girls went into the cabin for their food break, they could smell fish. There was nothing unusual in that as they had all been handling the fish boxes themselves. But the following day the smell was still there and getting stronger. They moved the lockers and table out of the cabin, scrubbed the place out and put down disinfectant. All to no avail. The smell remained and was getting worse. Again, they gave the place a good going over, humping the table in last but not thinking to look under it. By the time they did discover the source, the fish head was in one hell of a state!

The Waiting Room Clock

The Cymer Afan waiting room clock, a wooden wall clock, stopped some time in 1947. The station master made arrangements for it to be sent back to Swindon to be repaired. First of all, he had to send for a wooden packing case in which to send it. Eventually, after about a month, the repaired clock arrived back in Cymer. The station master told the porter and me – I was a lad porter at the time – to put the clock back on the waiting room wall above the fireplace at a height of about ten feet from the floor. We got the station stepladder out, placed it ready by the wall and my mate climbed up it with the clock. I thought it was a bit pointless having me standing there just holding the ladder, so I told him, "I'll be in the booking office if you want me." Once in the booking office, the next thing I heard was the ladder slipping. I rushed to the door to see my mate suspended in midair, trying to hold on to the clock. The clock fell down and smashed to smithereens and all the pieces had to be gathered up and sent back to Swindon to be repaired again! My mate didn't hurt himself thankfully.

A few years later the wooden waiting room clock from the other waiting room on Cymer General platform was stolen. It was never found.

Ben Blunt

Prior to around 1957, a workmen's train left Aberavon Town at 21.45 on Mondays to Fridays. This train would terminate at Cymer Afan. It was shunted into the loop, the engine then ran around and after the passage of the down parcels' train, it was propelled out of the loop and back to the down-platform to make the 23.25 workmen's train to Aberavon Town. During the time the train was at Cymer, the train members of staff would come up to the Afan signal box for a cup of tea and a chat. The guard of this train was a Mr Ben Jones, who had been a goods' guard for years at Aberavon Town. He went under the name of 'Ben Blunt' owing to his frankness. He had told us that he had decided to apply for the post of passenger guard and in due course he was notified that he'd been successful. The driver said, "You'll have a new uniform now, Ben, with a lot of gold braid on it. It will take a few weeks yet though." "When I do get it, I'll let you know," said Ben. Eventually, it arrived. "Well, why the hell didn't you wear it today, then?" asked the driver. "No," said Ben, "I'm going to leave it until Monday. Start the week off properly." The boys were satisfied – now they knew when Ben's big day would be. "I bet you'll look a real swank, Ben, putting all us lot in the shade!"

The following Monday afternoon, my father, W.J. Morgan, who was the signalman at Cymer Afan box, went to work in his best suit, complete with kid gloves and a bowler hat with a gold-braided station master's badge pinned on it. When the 13.50 workmen's from Aberavon to Blaenrhondda arrived at Cymer to the sound of exploding detonators, the driver got off the engine. He too was dressed up, in top hat and tails. My father was on the platform to give the tokens and he said to the driver, "I think this calls for a pint!" and over the Refresh they went. But Ben, momentarily lost for words, never got out of the van but shouted after them, "You pair of b★★★★★★s!" but with a grin on his face.

Animal tales

The afternoon shift porters would sometimes lock a sheep inside the goods' shed overnight – providing there was no food stuff in there – just for devilment. When the morning shift came on and they slid the door across, they'd have the shock of their lives as the sheep bolted passed them to freedom.

On one particular Thursday in 1955 the lampman, on returning from changing the lamp at Blaengwynfi down distant signal – which was positioned a quarter of a mile inside Blaenrhondda tunnel, mentioned to the signalman and me, "A lovely goose been killed about 100 yards inside the tunnel." So, my mate went in with an old coat to wrap around the carcass, came back out with it and took it underneath the box to feather it. "That's my meat sorted for the weekend!" I don't know how long the owner spent looking for his lost goose. Its death had been instantaneous, its head being neatly cut off by the engine wheel. A butcher couldn't have done a better job!

A slight bit of poaching

It was the duty of the afternoon signalman at Blaengwynfi to light a Tilley lamp and put it on the lampost 50 yards below the signal box before it got dark. This was to enable the goods' guard to see where he was walking when going to apply the wagon brakes on a down coal train, before going down the gradient. While lighting this lamp one day, as I walked to and from the post, I looked in the river that ran alongside, I wondered if there were any trout in it. Sure enough, there were and they stayed where they were while I put my hand in and tickled them. I thought, this is better than catching them with a fishing rod – and a lot quicker! But there was one fish I couldn't catch. I tried for weeks but had no luck. The water from the Blaengwynfi end of the tunnel and the two water columns was drained through pipes which ran between the up and down tracks of the station and eventually into a trench, and then into the river. This trench was approximately three feet deep and two feet wide, with about a foot of water in it. I noticed that whenever I went near the trench, the trout always disappeared up the pipe and all I could see of it was its tail fin. I had tried to catch it with a night line but with no success. I had thought of stunning it with a railway detonator – but I had no means of detonating it underwater. Another idea I had was to put worms in the bottom of a big glass jar, wind wires round the top with the ends pointing into the jar, lay it on its side in the water, thereby enticing the fish in but preventing it getting back out. Again, no luck. Then I thought of the Tilley lamp; so, one night shift I armed myself with a slat of wood, three feet by three inches, from an orange box that I found, and the lamp and set out. When I got to the trench the trout was outside the pipe. I transfixed it with the light, pushed down with the piece of wood and caught my trout by the tail! But now came the difficult part, which I had not worked out. How could I hold the trout by the wood and, at the same time, dispose of the lamp, get down on my knees, roll up my sleeve, plunge my arm in the water, lean forward, maintain my balance and feel around in the dark to grip the slippery fish. At best I would end up doing a nosedive into the water and spend the rest of the shift soaked to the skin. I had to let it go again!

A few weeks later, when I got home from afternoon shift, I noticed that my wife had a hairnet on over her rollers. A brainwave – that's what I needed to catch it with, a net! So I took it to work on the next night shift I spent at Blaengwynfi box. I cut a piece of signal wire, threaded it through the perimeter of the hairnet and went fishing with that and my lamp. Down at the trench, it was just a matter of scooping the fish out of the water. Success! Strangely, after I'd caught it I began to wish I hadn't as I'd had so much fun trying. But that feeling didn't last long. It was about fourteen inches long. Not bad! My wife and I enjoyed it the following day.

Keeping an eye out

One of the porters at Cymer was courting a girl from the village whose home was close to one of the railway signals worked from the General signal box. When the porter would spot the girl's mother catching a train to go shopping – and knowing that her father was in work – he would approach the signalman to ask him to do him a favour, "If you should see either of her parents getting off a train, could you pull that signal a few times to give me a chance to get out of her house before they arrive? I'll leave the window open so we can hear the signal drop!"

Another signalman, when walking from Cymer General signal box to the booking office one night, noticed a courting couple by the wooden fence at the end of the station building. The blackout was in force at the time and the couple were taking advantage of it, kissing passionately, but innocently. He walked the mileage at the back of the building until he reached where the couple stood, put his hand through the paling fence and touched the girl's thigh. She gave her boyfriend a good slap on his face for his cheek!

Mr Harry Webb, who was a wagon repairer stationed at Glyncorrwg, had lost one eye in an accident while doing his job, and had a glass eye. One day, while having his food break in the wagon repair cabin with the rest of the boys who were working with him, he had a message from the station porter to say he was required on the telephone. Harry had not finished his food and had just poured himself a cup of tea. Before leaving the cabin to take the call, he removed his artificial eye, put it on the table by his sandwiches and said to it, "Now, I've got my eye on that lot until I get back!"

Some advice

One of my mates was getting married during the late 1940s and didn't want to start a family straight away. He came across an advert in one of the newspapers which said "Thinking of getting married? Do you want advice on contraception and family planning? Then write to 'Post Box 123', enclosing a stamped addressed envelope and a postal order for three shillings." For a week or more he waited in anticipation. Then his letter arrived. Inside was a short note with the advice to "Keep 'Toby' out!" The bloke who put the advert in the paper must have made a small fortune with that pearl of wisdom! There was no denying that my mate had received advice, it just wasn't the advice he wanted. Incidentally, he never did have children – though, as he said, it wasn't for want of trying as they would both have liked a family as the years went by.

Swing gates

One noticeable feature of the Rhondda and Swansea Bay Railway at Cymer Afan, which was erected to maintain their boundary across the Afan river, were the swing gates. One set was positioned below the Seven Arches viaduct and another crossing the river below Gelli tunnel, their purpose being to prevent animals wading through the river and gaining access to the railway lines. These must have been installed in conjunction with the Great Western Railway, as their lines were involved also.

The Afan river is fast-flowing, quick to rise and quick to fall after heavy rain. Six-feet-high brick pillars had been built on each side of the river at these points and pitch-pine beams that spanned the water were laid to rest on them. Below the beams, four gates consisting of pitch-pine hanging slats were hinged to a metal bar. They moved to and fro with the movement of the water rising to float horizontally when it was in full flood, and returning to their vertical position when the water level dropped again.

Crossing the river by means of balancing on the pine beams, arms outstretched, was a challenge to every youngster in the village!

Graig crash

One day *c.*1969 the Cymer pilot, drawn by a diesel shunter of the type nicknamed 'the Iron Lung' (and sometimes 'Teddy Bears', though why I don't know) had finished its work for the day at Avon Colliery and brakes had been applied on the un-fitted train, which was fully loaded. It was a fine day and the guard and the carriage and wagon examiner were on the brake van (with the gradient about 1 in 35). The guard gave right of way to the driver to start off. As soon as the train had pulled clear of the National Coal Board line, the shunter reversed to a safety point to protect the British Railways line and had to run quickly to get on the brake van to join the other two men. After a short while, when the train was approaching the stone-built over-bridge at St John's, one said to the others, "Don't you think we're going too fast?" but the guard replied, "Oh, don't worry. He's a good driver," but applied the van handbrake full on – just in case.

When they were on the straight and looking forward towards the diesel engine, they suddenly noticed the loco men jumping off, so the three of them thought they had better do likewise! The result was that the diesel engine hit the runaway stop-block, and came off the road with loaded wagons of coal piling up on top of each other. One hell of a mess with coal all over the place. The train's staff immediately went to protect the obstruction with detonators. Mr Robert Morgan (who was the carriage wagon examiner on the brake van, and making his way back to Cymer from the colliery) said that as soon as the people living in the nearby houses above heard the crash, they ran down to see if anyone was injured and needed help. Luckily, no-one was hurt apart from shock and bruises. Shortly afterwards they returned with flasks of hot tea, which were very much appreciated.

In the aftermath, some of the coal spillage found its way into the coal houses of Heol y Felin and Heol Treharne. Every cloud has a silver lining!

The miniature glasshouse

Idris was a good gardener. I wasn't. I grew, successfully, kidney beans, *shibwns* (spring onions), radishes and lettuces and for my wife chrysanthemums, sweet peas and carnations. There my interest and capability ended. One day Idris gave me some small, sweet tomatoes he'd grown. They were delicious and I told him so. "You should try growing them, then," he said. "It's easy." "I haven't got a glasshouse Id, and no room to put one." "Get a small, moveable one mate. In fact, I've got one you can have." A few days later, a cardboard parcel arrived at the box addressed to me. It was about 18 inches square with a short note attached. "Good luck with your tomatoes John – Idris." I opened the box, removed a layer of straw and took out the damned miniature glasshouse.

Refreshment Rooms, Cymer Afan

The Refreshment Rooms were built about 1887, by the Rhondda and Swansea Bay Railway to serve passengers that were waiting for or changing trains at Cymer which, at one time, was an important junction. There were very few village stations which could boast such facilities. If one looked at the railway timetable, right up until the station closed, Cymer Afan was always shown as having a Refresh (catered by outsiders). It was leased to Wm. Hancock, the Brewery. (The date of Wm. Hancock taking over the lease can be worked out by looking back at the old timetables.) I can only remember beer being sold there, never any food or cups of tea. When I made enquiries, years ago, I was told you could get a snack and either a tea or coffee up until about 1924. It also had three bars. During the time Miss May Davies was landlady there, she called these bars the morning room, the public bar and the coffee room. Miss Davies had taken the licence over from her father and had been in the Refresh for years. At the first sign of a row starting or if anyone used bad language, she'd tell them to get out and out they'd go! She finished there through illness in 1960, at the age of about 75, when the licence was taken over by Mr G. Jones. The Refresh was the last dressed-stone building to be built by the Rhondda and Swansea Bay Railway in the Afan Valley. Blaengwynfi East box, the stations at Pontrhydyfen, Cwmafan and Aberavon Town were also built of dressed-stone. All the stations that were built later were made of wood and corrugated sheets, presumably to save money.

By the side of the Refresh (c.1943) there was, at one time, a wooden cottage. This had originally been built by the side of the railway, near Gelli tunnel, to accommodate the railway navvies while they were building the Rhondda and Swansea Bay line. A hundred yards towards the Cymer side of Gelli tunnel, there is a flat piece of ground where part of the stone foundation can still be seen on the right-hand side, but not for much longer as it's quickly being covered up by overgrowth. Mr David Jones, an old signalman, told me that around 1910 this wooden building was dismantled and removed on railway trolleys to be rebuilt near the site that is now the telephone exchange. It was called Station Cottage and was once occupied by a Mr Sheppard, signalman at Cymer Afan.

Beer for the Refresh came by rail up until about 1956. It would arrive in a goods' van from Swansea and be put off in Cymer Yard. On a Thursday, the Cymer pilot would pick the van up and take it over the Rhondda and Swansea Bay railway to stand on the up-line outside the Refresh, ready to be unloaded. Then it was all hands on deck as the railway staff – from the pilot, shunter, Cymer Afan signalman, the fireman and porter and even female workers when they were working at Cymer – would unload the beer and cellar it. The two lad porters would be behind the bar, putting the bottles on the shelves – and making sure there was always a full bottle going out with the empty case! It was a work of art as we all rolled the barrels down the platform ramp and did a U-turn to the cellar door. Everyone who helped would get a free pint or a packet of Woodbine cigarettes from Miss Davies, and a full bottle or two to share out afterwards. It was a good system, benefiting everybody and she was very thankful to us all.

She would often also call us in for a chat or to help with an odd job or two, such as repairing the lino (which was identical to that in the signal box and the station) on innumerable times, her electric fire – which was as old as the hills, or put new washers in the taps and cistern. May Davies liked a bit of a lie-in in the mornings as she got older. The paperboy delivered her newspaper about 07.30 which didn't go unnoticed by the Cymer Afan signalman who, knowing full well that she wouldn't be up until around 09.30, would remove the paper from the gap under the door with a hooked piece of wire and read it between trains! This went on for quite a while until one morning, Miss Davies, up earlier than usual, bent to pick up the paper just as it began to slide out from under the door. But she took it all in good part.

About 1948, Mr Ossie White (who had been a shunter during the war but had to revert back to his porter's job when one of the shunters returned from the forces) thought that it was not the railway staff's job to cellar the beer. Following his advice, we all refused to do it. So, the next time, May asked some of her regular customers to carry it in from the platform and paid them, before reporting the staff's refusal to Wm. Hancock, the brewers. The following week, the station master told us that we had to do the work as Wm. Hancock had signed an agreement with British Railways divisional office in Swansea High Street, with Miss Davies paying them three shillings and ten pence per week for cellaring the beer. From that day on the only ones who were given a free pint were the foreman or porter, who took the book over for her to sign for the beer and pay the 3/10d. Thanks to Ossie, we'd all cut our noses off to spoil our faces!

My father told me that at one time the beer used to come from Burton-on-Trent. One night, when the van of beer was in Cymer yard, some men had gone underneath it and with a brace and bit and had drilled through the wooden floor and kept going until they had drilled through a wooden barrel, then filled buckets with the beer that poured out!

When one of the railwaymen who worked in the Cymer area retired, we would make a collection for him and have the presentation over at the Refresh. During the severe winter of 1963/64, the water mains there froze with the result that they didn't have water for twelve weeks. To get over this problem, Winston Edwards, the ganger, and I used to put an empty barrel on the train and take it up to Blaengwynfi station to fill it with water, as Cymer Station had none. Later on, we borrowed garden hosepipes from different people and joined them together so that we could cross over the breadth of seven railway lines plus the garden of Mr and Mrs Viv Jones of Margam Street to fill some empty barrels in the cellar of the Refresh with water from that house, to keep it ticking over – necessity being the mother of invention. Mr and Mrs Denzil Jones, the then landlord and landlady, gave Winston and I a pint glass each and told us to help ourselves to the beer. So, while the barrels filled up with water – which took a long time – we both filled up with beer. Den would come down to the cellar and if our glasses weren't full would tell us to "fill them up, boys". As a result of the barrels taking so long to fill, as water pressure was low, I was about three hours late going home and fell asleep shortly afterwards, waking up to find that my wife had eaten my dinner as it was four hours or more since she'd had her own – she was so tired of waiting for me. So I had to make do with some corned beef and chips!

Say nothing's the best

If we had a derailment of a wagon or, say, one pair of wheels of a loco, we would do our best to rerail them without anyone knowing. We would use the rerailing ramps, wooden packing, pit props etc. We would only call the break-down unit out if it was too bad for the local boys to deal with. By doing it ourselves, it saved a lot of writing out of reports and visits to the superintendent in Swansea High Street. The station master always made sure he was not around when we were rerailing!

We knew we were right

The track in the Treorchy tunnel had been ripped up. We couldn't believe it. Allegedly, it was dangerous. Bullshit! No-one would accept that, especially the workforce. Steve Radmore and I were having a few pints in the Refresh and discussing this. We decided to walk through it there and then, to prove it to ourselves. The powers that be were bloody idiots to come to that decision. We walked, we talked, we stopped to point out places and walked on again. There was daylight ahead. We had reached the end. Out we came, but not in Treorchy. We were back in Cymer. During our heated conversation about those bloody idiots we had turned without realising it, and were back where we had started!

Every cloud…

During that first Christmas after the ravenous raping and ripping up of our beloved railways (which just broke our hearts) by the scavenger scrap merchants, a group of us got together and arranged a Boxing Day walk along the local tracks that once existed. It developed into an annual event involving a different section of track every year. Depending on the distance of these destinations, we would hire a minibus to either take us or fetch us home and would stop at some point for a meal and a pint or two – or maybe more! Pure nostalgia, purified with alcohol! We drew up the following rules and regulations for membership of this club:

The Cymer Afan and District Railway Appreciation Society

(founded 1982)

Incorporating the industrial, archaeological, antiquity, scouting, rambling, Morris dancing, bird watching and 4x2 fraternities.

The object of this society shall be not to take life too seriously. i.e.: soap operas, cowboy films, party politics, the *F.T.* and Dow Jones index, whether it was a castle or a class 8 on the last workmen's train from North Rhondda.

It is the duty of all members to watch and be guided by *Last of the Summer Wine* and to remember that we are 'only passing through'. As Isambard Kingdom Brunel would say, "*Nil desperandum*", or in these days, "*Illegitimi non carborundum*".

Discussions over the last few years have been on the following:
- Who the hell planned the new fire station at Cymer and why?
- Why did they pull Pontrhydyfen bridge down? And then put one back.
- Whose idea was it to put the new school where it is?
- The advantage of the paper kettle.
- The advantage of hook–and–wheel transport.
- How did Pythagaros work out his theorem before even seeing a steam locomotive?
- The 3–4–5 method.
- Where were *you* when they closed Duffryn Rhondda?

The Final Word

When one station master left after securing promotion in 1955, he told his successor:

> You never know what's going to happen next with the staff up in this valley. They're all bloody comedians, every last one of them. There's a nest of them up here, and they're a law unto themselves. You never know what they'll get up to next! Still, having said that, I can't pick a bloody fault with the way they carry out their work and they know all the rules and regulations. But they've also got a few of their own!

Who could wish for a better testimonial?

A humorous war-time story set in the Welsh valleys

olicka bolicka

& Pink Bluebells

Sheila Morgan

y Lolfa

£7.95

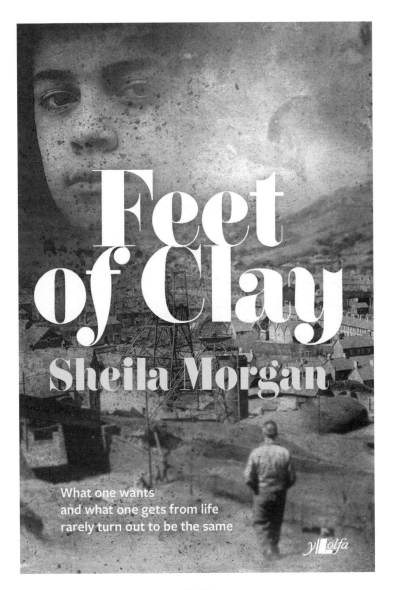

Feet
of Clay

Sheila Morgan

What one wants
and what one gets from life
rarely turn out to be the same

y Lolfa

£7.95

CHRIS NEEDS

highs and lows

Tales from the rollercoaster life of
the legendary radio presenter

Edited by Gabe Cameron

y Lolfa

£9.95

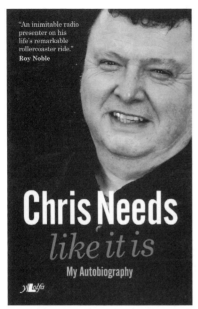

£9.95

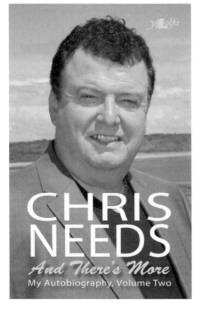

£9.95